SEW

fabulous

SEW *fabulous*

Inspiring ideas to bring the joy
of sewing to your home

STUART HILLARD

CONTENTS

Introduction 6

All the Trimmings: Software and Hardware 10

The Basic Skills: Everything you Need to Know 28

Patterns 56

Inspired Entrance 60

Liberated Lounging 76

Rustic Kitchen 92

Dressed-up Dining 120

Bedroom Bliss 138

Garden Graces 172

Gorgeous Gifts 196

Glossary 216

Stockists 218

Index 220

Acknowledgements 223

THE GOLDEN RULES OF SUCCESSFUL SEWING

Forgive me for calling them rules; call it friendly advice if you prefer. There are a few things I have learned along the way that will lead you to successful sewing; the rest is just practice.

GOLDEN RULE NUMBER 1 – *Read the instructions*

Read them right through from beginning to end, then read them again. I have learned that in sewing, as in life generally, some of the early steps don't make a lot of sense until later, then everything clicks into place. We have all experienced that 'aha' moment in life, haven't we, when suddenly things make sense? Read the instructions from start to finish and you'll get that 'aha' moment before you even start. What a great beginning!

GOLDEN RULE NUMBER 2 – *Use fabric you love*

Great sewing is like great cooking; use good-quality ingredients, treat them simply and just let that quality shine. Use fabrics that make your heart sing, allow the beauty of the fabric to shine through and you will love the finished article. I promise!

GOLDEN RULE NUMBER 3 – *Cut and sew accurately*

If your cutting out is wobbly and your seams have more contours than Mount Fuji, your pieces won't fit together! As the saying goes: measure twice, cut once. If you struggle to sew straight, accurate seams, mark them lightly with a pencil; most people can sew accurately if they have a line to follow.

GOLDEN RULE NUMBER 4 – *Get tooled up for the job*

You don't need a lot of special equipment to make the projects in this book but the right tools really do make the job easier, so no cutting out with the kids' scissors please! Whatever you do, always use a new needle for each new project and get yourself some good pins (and use them!).

GOLDEN RULE NUMBER 5 – *Create the right environment*

Make yourself a nice drink (tea, milk, no sugar, if you're asking), get comfy, make sure the lighting is adequate and you've got some space to work in.

And most importantly . . .

GOLDEN RULE NUMBER 6 – *Enjoy yourself!*

INTRODUCTION

Welcome! It's time we went from 'So Drab' to 'Sew Fab(ulous)'!

I'm so glad you have bought my first ever book, *Sew Fabulous*. Clearly you love fabric and want to get creative with it and that's why I wrote this book – to celebrate fabulous fabric and to inspire you to make your home uniquely yours. Fabric crafting for the home is easy, straightforward, requires no previous experience and adds individuality and value to your living space. Many of us rent our homes or only stay for a few years before we move on and fabric crafts are the perfect way to bring colour and pattern to the home without making any permanent changes. Better still, these projects are completely portable so we can take them to our next home and make it fabulous too. The fabric crafts in this book are graded from Easy to Challenging but even the more advanced projects are achievable for the novice, with just a little extra time and care. Crafting with fabric is not a hardship; it is exciting, expressive and fun.

I have always loved fabric and thread, yarn, sewing, buttons and trims, but the first person who really inspired me to be creative and enjoy fabric crafts was a wonderful junior schoolteacher called Miss Jenkins. Miss Jenkins wore sparkly green eyeshadow and lots of silver jewellery; it was the 1970s and there was that whole craft revival thing going on.

We had a spinning wheel in the classroom and Miss Jenkins taught us to spin; it was like pure magic to me, watching the wheel turn and yarn (or 'wool' as everything yarn-like was called then) appeared. That year we knitted, we sewed, we made macramé pot holders and odd lumpy weavings. Miss Jenkins and I (the rest of the class just disappeared) spent that year together making beautiful things. She started my journey into the wonderful world of sewing and creativity and I'm very, very grateful to her.

Everyone who comes to sewing does so for their own reasons. I sew because I have to: it's the easiest and most accessible way I've ever found to express my thoughts, feelings and imagination. I sew because it makes me very, very happy and I sew because I want lots of gorgeous pieces in my home. As a child I asked my mother the same question and she gave the same answer: I sew because I have to. She sewed because it was cheaper to; in fact, it was the only way we could afford a new pair of curtains or a cushion. As soon as the lean times ended my mother put her needle away and it has never reappeared. When I left university and set up my first home I did not go out and buy curtains – I went out and bought the things I needed to make the curtains – I did what my mother would have done in my position. The difference was that I believed I would enjoy the process, and enjoy it I did. So much so that when the curtains were finished, then came cushions, then a quilt for my bed and the joy of crafting with fabric had begun.

As part of a generation who didn't really learn to sew, I was glad I had the influences that I did. My contemporaries didn't want to be unique; we all wanted to be the same as everybody else and my goodness we got what we wanted. But now times have changed and we are all craving to be unique. A sewing revolution has begun and many of us are discovering the sheer joy and delight to be gained from making something that no one else has. We want homes that reflect our personalities a bit more. Well, the great news is that the skills needed to make the projects in this book are not hard ones and you certainly do not need a lifetime of experience to achieve perfect results.

HOW TO USE THIS BOOK

The first chapter, All the Trimmings, is a run-through of all the equipment and materials you might need for the projects here. Whether you're a seasoned sewer or a total newcomer, have a read of this chapter before you make anything – just to refresh your knowledge. Products and equipment change and in recent years there have been some big changes in the technology available to sewers. The good news is that there has never been a better time to sew; the market is full of products that make the job easier and more successful even for the absolute beginner. If you can't find the proper tools it is often possible to improvise. For example, I do not own a 'point turner' (for pushing out the corners on cushions and the like) but I do have a kitchen drawer full of chopsticks that do the job just as well. Be inventive and do it your way. If the end result is the same does it matter if you do it your way? Exactly!

The Basic Skills chapter is full of all the technical know-how and basic methods you will need to complete all the projects in this book and more. Don't be alarmed by this chapter; there is nothing scary in those pages – it's all very friendly and is there to refresh your knowledge or supplement what you already know.

If you've never sewn before, you definitely want to read the chapter thoroughly and don't be afraid to practise individual skills in isolation before you use them in a project. Every step is fun and your skills will quickly build. Throughout the book I have provided you with both metric and imperial conversions, but be sure to consistently follow one or the other, don't mix and match!

The rest of the book is organised into chapters relating to rooms in the typical home: kitchen, dining room, bedroom and so on. Each chapter, or room, has its own 'crafts', which I have made specifically for that space. But don't fear, the crafts are portable! Very few of the projects are limited to use in only one room, and I hope that you will see the possibilities in each craft and transfer it to a place that works for you. Many of the projects include a Project Variation so that with just a few tweaks, those dining room napkins can become casual, everyday kitchen napkins.

The colour schemes are all completely versatile; I have chosen fabrics and colours that create a 'look' that you can reproduce if you wish or transfer to a different room if you prefer and there will almost certainly be some looks that you will completely reject. That's a good thing! You have your own style; run with it. Try to see through my colour and fabric choices to see the project itself. The Project Variations, where provided, will give you some ideas for variations of colour and design.

Any project could work for you if you just remember Golden Rule Number 2 (Use fabric you love).

TIPS FOR THE BEGINNER

If you have little or no sewing experience, rest assured you are in safe hands! I understand better than most what it's like to feel nervous and out of your depth. Once you've got the basic skills (and they are very basic!) you can tackle anything if you take your time and drink plenty of milky tea.

Read the first few chapters of the book carefully and keep referring back to them often. Start with some of the 'No Sew' projects or really simple sewing projects first. I've designed these projects for you to need very little skill or equipment (often not even a sewing machine). Avoid things with zips and bindings to start with. Keep to the really basic projects and you'll enjoy success the first time; buoyed by this success you can then tackle something a little harder. If you start with the hardest projects and get stuck you might be put off. You may want to make the huge bed quilt first but take my advice and start with a cushion. You'll get it done in very little time, have a fabulous cushion to admire and you'll feel like a sewing superstar!

LEVELS OF DIFFICULTY

I've given each project in this book a difficulty rating:

EASY [NO SEW]	**EASY**	**EASY/ MEDIUM**
MEDIUM	**MEDIUM / CHALLENGING**	**CHALLENGING**

Each project will have earned its rating for a number of reasons: it might be the length of time you need to complete the project, or the number of different steps or stages it takes. A project might be labelled Challenging because it has a zip but if you find zips easy, the project won't be too challenging for you. The best way to decide if a project is for you is to read through the stages and see if there are any steps that are new or difficult.

I hope this will be just a starting point for you in unlocking your creativity and building your sewing skills. I'm with you every step of the journey . . . we can even hold hands!

Stuart
xxx

ALL THE TRIMMINGS

SOFTWARE AND HARDWARE

In this chapter you'll find all the important information about the sort of fabrics, threads, interfacings, fusibles and trims that I love to use. It's not an exhaustive list of course, but it's the fabrics and products that I have found give me the best results with minimal fuss. Technology has moved on incredibly since I started sewing and there is a whole range of exciting new products to discover. They make our craft easier and more successful . . . what's not to love about that?

Fabrics 12

Thread 14

Accessories 16

Fusibles 16

Sewing Machine 18

Stitches 20

Interchangeable Feet 22

Other Useful Kit 24

SOFTWARE

FABRICS, THREADS, FUSIBLES AND OTHER GOOD STUFF

FABRICS

CRAFT-WEIGHT COTTON

For the majority of my projects I like to use 100 per cent craft-weight cotton. It's 100–110cm (40–42in) wide, medium-weight and comes in such an enormous range of colours, patterns and styles that there is quite literally something for everybody. It is perfect for patchwork and quilting, table linens, bed linens and bags. I use it for lined curtains and blinds and for light/medium-use upholstery.

CALICO

The perfect cotton fabric for making linings, backings and cushion inners, it comes in wide widths, is inexpensive and durable.

CANVAS AND DECKCHAIR CANVAS

The former is brilliant for robust outdoor cushions, beanbags and aprons, the latter is perfect for revamping tired garden furniture and bags.

UPHOLSTERY-WEIGHT FABRIC

Cotton, linen and mixtures of the two are the perfect choice for robust heavy curtains, blinds and upholstery, but the choice of colours and designs is more limited than craft-weight fabrics. Mix upholstery basics with craft-weight cotton accessories for an exciting combination.

LAMINATES AND OILCLOTH

Oiled or plastic-coated cotton fabrics can be fairly thick and sturdy so are great for table covers. The thinner variety has great drape ability for shower curtains, picnic blanket backings, bags/linings, etc.

WOOL

I have recently discovered British Wool and I think I'm in love! It's easy to work with and doesn't fray much, which makes it a great choice for all kinds of home-styling projects. The best thing about it is there are some really innovative mills doing exciting new colours and weaves so the possibilities are expanding all the time.

SCRAPS

Inevitably when you cut fabric you end up with some scraps . . . please don't throw them away! Keep in mind that those little offcuts and strips you were about to trash cost just as much as the whole piece of fabric. Sew thin strips and squares together using a neutral thread to make 'new' fabric and use it to make cushions or, for example, the Scented Scrap Heart (see page 202), Patchwork Eye Mask (see page 156) or little bags. It's a good idea to use fabrics of a similar weight and composition (wool with wool, cotton with cotton, etc.) if you can.

THREAD

I use cotton thread, or more typically, polyester general-purpose sewing thread for most of my construction and piecing work. The most important thing with thread is that the thread is of really good quality, smooth and long staple. Do not be lured by cheap threads; they will not sew well or last – remember, the thread is literally what holds everything together! Cheap threads produce lots of lint which will clog up your machine and result in poor stitch quality. Really cheap thread will break often, give poor stitch definition and can even damage your fabrics.

Coats Dual Duty 6970 Army Drab is my favourite grey/green for general piecing and the colour blends with most of the fabrics I use. For topstitching and quilting, I generally use the same kind of thread in a matching or blending colour as the fabric, although there are many kinds of thread out there aimed specifically at quilting. For machine appliqué, I like to use a regular-weight cotton or polyester all-purpose thread in a matching colour, although I do sometimes use a contrast colour for special effect.

ACCESSORIES

TRIMS

I'm a recent convert to trims – pompom, bobble, tassel, ric rac and braid, beaded or fringed. A bit of well-placed trim can elevate a project to starry heights . . . too much and you'll be giving your project away to a drag queen . . . unless you are a drag queen!

BUTTONS

I don't do a lot of buttonholes (there are none in any of the projects in this book) but I do like buttons and there are plenty of those here. They make great trims and embellishments on cushions and bags. I love buttons that are covered with your own choice of fabric; they look so smart and give a very professional look to home décor.

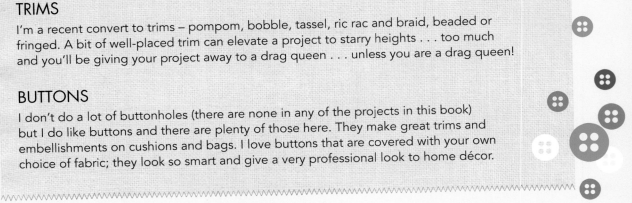

FUSIBLES

INTERFACING

Interfacing is a special kind of fabric that is ironed or sewn to the back of flimsy fabrics to give them more body and weight. Every haberdashery or fabric shop will have a few rolls of rather thin, usually white, gauzy material that looks like a cross between fabric and paper.

Interfacing comes in three weights: light, medium and stiff or heavy. I use light- and medium-weight for added body and a heavyweight for sturdy fabric bags, boxes and baskets. I prefer to use fusible interfacing (the stuff you iron on) but you can use the sew-on variety for most of the projects if you prefer.

FUSIBLE WEB

Fusible webs are essentially a fine mist of glue sprayed onto a paper backing. Most of us have used this stuff at some point, usually bought in small packages in a haberdashery or general store. The type most of us are familiar with comes in the form of a 2.5cm- (1in) wide tape, which is used for hemming trousers and skirts instead of sewing. The tape is placed on the fabric, the hem is folded over the tape and heat is applied with an iron to melt the glue and literally stick the fabrics together. Genius and a great product for those No Sew projects!

If you look in larger fabric shops or online you will find this sort of fusible web in large sheets and this is great for fusible appliqué. The shape you want to appliqué is drawn onto the paper backing and cut out roughly, then ironed to the wrong side of the chosen fabric, cut out neatly and ironed onto the project. The edges of this fusible appliqué are usually finished with a straight, zigzag or blanket stitch. Some modern fusible webs do not need stitching and are still machine washable. Not all fusible webs are the same so check the manufacturer's instructions.

QUILT WADDING

Sometimes called batting, this material comes in packages or off the roll and is available in a number of different widths. Cotton, polyester and cotton/poly blends are all easy to find but you may also come across bamboo (very eco-friendly), recycled cotton/poly, wool or silk. Cotton and cotton blends are the easiest to use and wash well. They are suitable for quilts and quilted cushions, place mats, bags, wall hangings and accessories. I would recommend thermal insulating wadding for hot pads, trivets, oven mitts and picnic/shopping totes; it's also a very good choice for place mats and table runners.

QUILT BASTING SPRAY

This is a spray adhesive, used for fusing the backing, wadding and top layers of a quilt together prior to quilting and therefore saving the laborious process of pinning or basting the layers together. It's also brilliant for holding layers together for other projects like bags or seat covers before you sew or staple in place. Keep an eye out for fusible quilt wadding too: this is pre-treated with fusible on both sides and just needs ironing to the backing and front of the quilt before quilting.

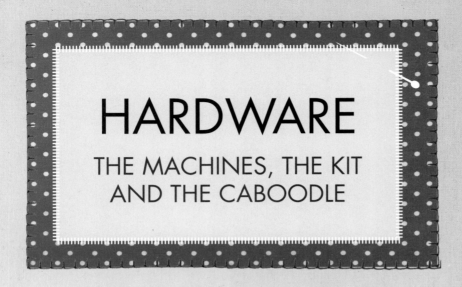

HARDWARE
THE MACHINES, THE KIT
AND THE CABOODLE

SEWING MACHINE

I spend at least as much time with my sewing machine as I do with my significant other, so unsurprisingly, I shopped around and found the best one available. I would strongly recommend you do the same – you are going to be together for a long time!

Sewing machines come in both manual and computerised types and, unlike relationships, they are both incredibly easy to understand. But remember, they come with a manual for a reason. Read it! This is no time to go all butch and jump in with both feet. Think of all those first- and second-date questions you'd ask a potential partner . . . get to know your sewing machine and it will reward you with a fruitful partnership. Yes, sometimes strong words are needed and my partner does ask me, when the air is blue, if I really enjoy sewing. I tell him, yes, I love it, but sometimes my machine and I have issues we need to straighten out.

With the projects in this book in mind specifically, and sewing in mind generally, your sewing machine needs to perform the basic stitches on page 20. You should also be able to drop or cover the feed dogs (those little teeth under the needle that feed the fabric through) for free-motion machine quilting and sewing on buttons. Check that you know how to do this on your machine. If in doubt, read the manual! If you've lost the manual, have a look online.

It is hugely helpful if you can move the position of your needle – this will enable you to sew seams of different widths while still using the edge of your presser foot as a guide. This makes for very accurate seam allowances. If you can't adjust the needle position don't worry. There are usually markings on the bed of your sewing machine to show different seam widths or you can mark commonly used widths with masking tape.

STITCHES

If your machine does nothing else aside from the stitches below, you will be able to tackle any of the projects in this book. However, there are a few other stitches that I use a lot and they are pretty common on most machines, so you shouldn't have any problems.

STRAIGHT STITCH

This is a no brainer – it's what sewing machines do and they all do it well. Use it for sewing hems and seams, patchwork, quilting, applying zips, piping, and topstitching.

ZIGZAG STITCH

Again, it's standard on pretty much every machine (apart from industrial machines). The zigzag stitch is great for neatening raw edges and finishing the edges of fusible appliqué. You can also use it for gathering frills (see Box-pleated Bed Valance, page 159) and as a decorative stitch.

OVERLOCK STITCH

This makes a really neat finish for the raw edges of seams and will make raw edges not only neater but also less likely to fray.

BLANKET STITCH

This is a decorative stitch, which mimics the look of a hand blanket stitch. I use this a lot for finishing the edges of fusible appliqué. If your machine doesn't have it, just use a straight stitch or zigzag.

AUTOMATIC BUTTONHOLE

Even quite basic sewing machines usually have an automatic buttonhole stitch. A special buttonhole foot is fixed on, you set the size of your button and the machine does the rest.

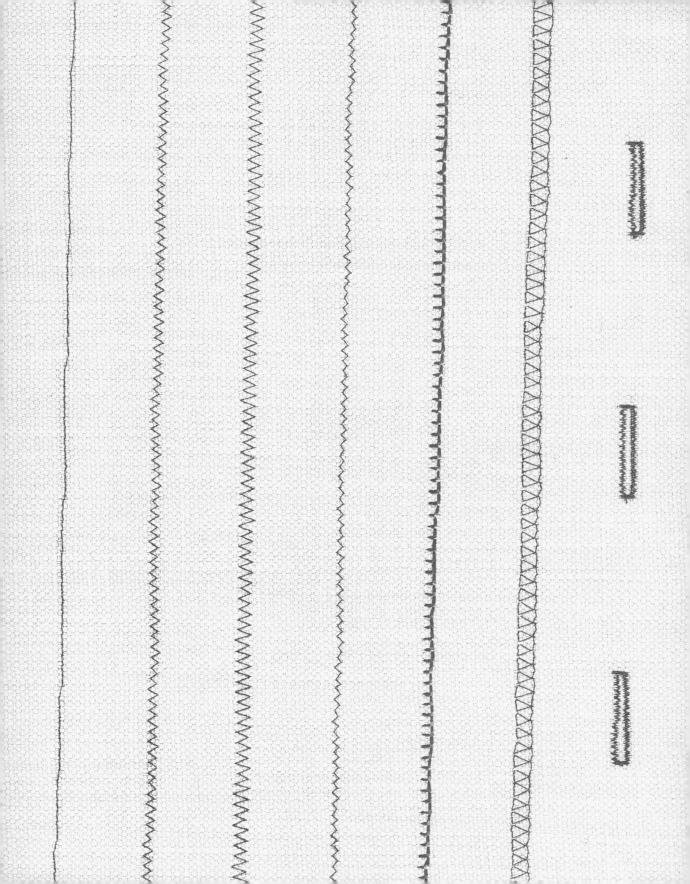

INTERCHANGEABLE FEET

Your sewing machine will come with a number of interchangeable feet, some may be optional extras. The ones I use most are:

STANDARD FOOT

This is the one that lives on your machine. Use it for general straight line, zigzag and decorative stitch sewing.

OPEN-TOE EMBROIDERY FOOT

As the name suggests, this foot has an open front, allowing you a much clearer view of what you're doing. Great for precision work and embroidery or fusible appliqué.

0.5CM (¼IN) PATCHWORK FOOT

For many of the projects you will use a 0.5cm (¼in) seam allowance so this foot, which you will normally need to purchase separately, is worth its weight in gold. Accurate seam allowances are essential if your patchwork is going to fit together so use the edge of the foot as a seam guide and you will always sew beautiful seams.

ZIPPER FOOT

This is a pretty standard piece of kit and should come with your machine. Its very narrow width allows you to sew really close to the teeth on zips but it's also brilliant for sewing on piping, braid, bobble trim and ric rac so it's worth digging out!

WALKING FOOT

A special foot that makes sewing long straight seams and lines of quilting a breeze. The walking foot or even feed foot ensures that bulky layers (like a quilt) won't shift while you're sewing, avoiding puckers and tucks. It's also useful for sewing oilcloth, laminates and leather if the mood takes you.

DARNING FOOT

This is another one used for quilting, combined with the feed dogs dropped or covered, for sewing in any direction and free-motion quilting.

One last thing, make sure your sewing machine is serviced regularly, cleaned and oiled as often as the manual (there, I said it again!) recommends. Care for your machine and you will be friends forever.

Open toe embroidery foot

Automatic buttonhole foot

Zipper foot

1/4" Patchwork foot

Walking foot

Overlock foot

Darning foot

OTHER USEFUL KIT

SEWING MACHINE NEEDLES

I use universal or microtex sharp needles for most projects as I generally use cotton fabrics. Sharp needles are good for machine appliqué and I tend to go for finer ones (10/70 or 12/80) as they leave less of a hole. Change your sewing machine needle every eight hours of sewing time – yes, you heard me! Don't just wait for it to break. Old needles lead to skipped and poor stitches and frustration.

HAND SEWING NEEDLES

I don't hand sew much so a pack of all-purpose hand sewing needles is usually sufficient for my needs. A darning needle is useful and a doll needle is brilliant for sewing through really thick layers.

PINS

I use long, fine pins, often labelled as lace or bridal pins. They don't leave holes and hold fabrics neatly together while you sew. Don't sew over pins! Sooner or later you will hit a pin with the needle and hear that stomach-churning crunch as your needle, and possibly your sewing machine, breaks. Just take the pins out before you get to them.

TAPE MEASURE

Essential but don't rely on it (sound familiar?) as the fabric variety can stretch over time.

TAILOR'S CHALK, MARKING PENCIL OR AIR-VANISHING PENS

All very useful for marking seams, button positions, darts, quilting lines, etc., but always check you can remove the marks by testing them on a scrap of the same fabric before you use them in your project.

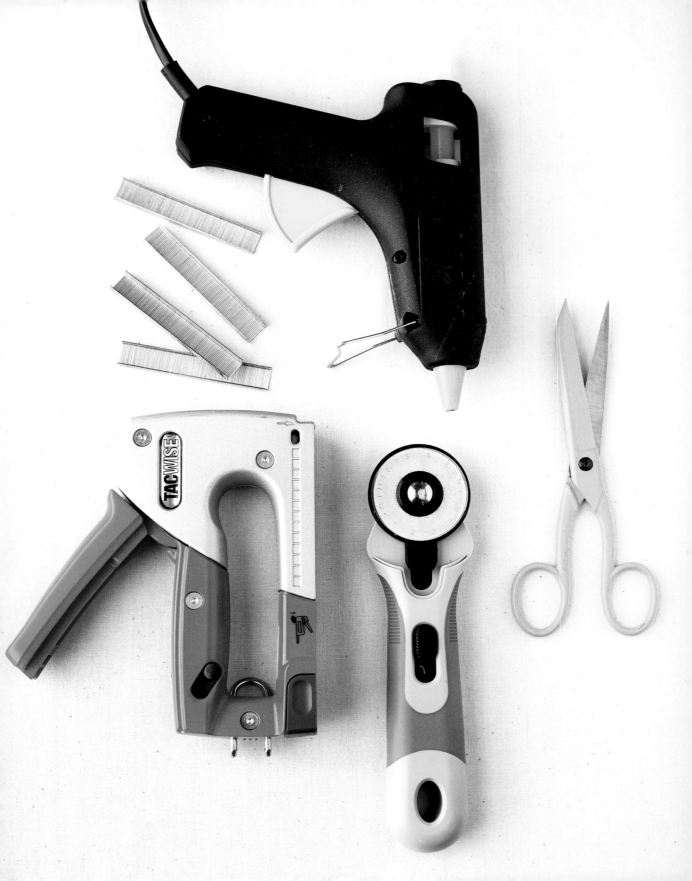

ROTARY CUTTER

These are used for cutting strips, squares, triangles and more. I couldn't work without mine – it's the most precise and accurate way to cut! Find them in quilting supplies shops and general haberdashery shops. Careful though; they can be very dangerous!

SCISSORS

Use a pair of large shears for big jobs, tiny ones with super sharp tips for appliqué and embroidery and a pair of thread snips – nothing blunts scissors like cutting thread (apart from cutting paper; we've all been shouted at for doing that, right?).

AND FOR THOSE NO SEW PROJECTS, I'D BE LOST WITHOUT:

A staple gun and staples, hot glue gun, upholstery tacks/pins and a hammer.

Stuart's Tip

- *You will also need a ruler and self-healing mat while using a rotary cutter. See page 31 for more information.*

- *When you're not using your rotary cutter, get into the habit of covering or retracting the blade every time. Safety first!*

THE BASIC SKILLS
EVERYTHING YOU NEED TO KNOW

You don't need decades of experience to make any of the projects in this book; with basic skills and great fabric, you should be able to make anything and be proud of your efforts. The basic skills found in this chapter will help you to tackle even the more complex items; but it would be sensible to start with the simpler projects if you are new to sewing. Keep this chapter to hand as well as your sewing machine manual, as every machine is slightly different. Once you've got the basics down, use those skills and my patterns as a springboard to expressing your own creativity!

Rotary Cutting 30

Stitching 33

Fusible Appliqué 34

Making and Applying Piping 37

Making Ties 40

Mitres 43

Inserting a Zip 44

Layering a Quilt Sandwich 46

Binding a Quilt 49

Making a Pieced Backing and Bagging Out 53

Making a Hanging Sleeve 54

Making an Envelope Back 55

ROTARY CUTTING

For the majority of my cutting I use the rotary cutting system. It's what I learned to use as a quilter and it works incredibly well for most home sewing applications. It's very accurate, fast and easy to master and consists of three very important pieces of equipment:

Rotary cutter: Essentially a circular blade mounted on a handle. As you push away, the blade rotates and cuts through up to eight layers of fabric. The most useful size to buy is one with a 45mm (1¾in) blade, although larger and smaller ones are available.

Rotary cutting ruler: A thick perspex ruler made specifically to use with a rotary cutter, it is marked in a grid of inches with smaller increments. The fabric is measured and cut using the ruler so no marking on shapes is necessary! Most also have lines showing the 45- and 60-degree angles. The most useful size to buy is 60x15cm (24x6in), although other sizes are available. It is used for straightening the edge, cutting strips on the straight of grain and the bias, and cutting rectangles, squares and triangles. Do not substitute any other kind of ruler, you must use one designed specifically for rotary cutters!

Self-healing mat: This goes on your work surface, the fabric and ruler go on top and then you cut. The mat protects your table from the blade and also has grid lines printed on it to help you measure and square up fabric. The most useful size to buy is 45x60cm (18x24in) – slightly bigger than A2.

STRAIGHTENING THE EDGE OF THE FABRIC

Start by straightening the edge of your fabric – fold it if necessary, selvedge to selvedge, and place it onto your mat with the fold at the bottom. Align the bottom of your ruler with the fold and hold the ruler firmly down with your left hand, push the blade of your rotary cutter out, position it against the ruler on the right-hand side (reverse if you are left-handed) and push the blade firmly up the edge of the ruler. You may need to move your left hand up the ruler to prevent the ruler slipping.

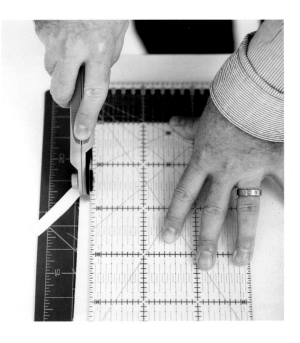

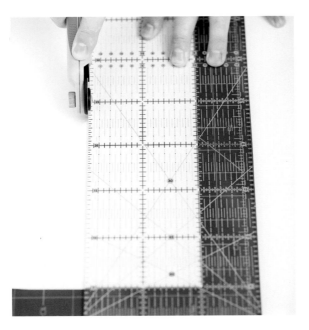

CUTTING STRIPS

Turn the mat a half turn so that the straightened edge is on the left and the fold is at the top. Position your ruler on top of the fabric with the top of the ruler lined up with the fold, and the width of strip you require under the ruler. Use the grid lines on the ruler to measure the strip width; the fabric to the right of the ruler is not covered and is spare. Position the cutter at the bottom of the ruler, blade out, and push to cut along the ruler edge. If you require more strips, simply move the ruler over to the required width and cut again.

CUTTING RECTANGLES, SQUARES AND TRIANGLES

Cut strips to the required width, then cut again into rectangles or squares. Cut rectangles or squares on the diagonal to make triangles.

CUTTING BIAS STRIPS FOR BINDING

Straighten the bottom edge of a square of fabric then place the 45-degree line on your ruler on this edge; the ruler will be placed across the fabric at an angle of 45 degrees, the true bias. Cut strips to the required width and join them with diagonal seams. Be careful when handling fabric cut on the bias as the edges will be very stretchy and can easily distort.

STITCHING

I don't use a lot of fancy stitches and, for the majority of the sewing that most of us want to do, we only really need the basic stitches done well.

STRAIGHT STITCHES

I mostly sew cotton, woven wool and linen, so a straight stitch is my absolute standard. For piecing and construction I use a stitch length of 2.5mm per stitch, and it's worth backstitching at the beginning and end of your stitching lines for added strength. For quilting and topstitching I generally like a slightly longer length stitch, 3.0–3.5mm (⅛in) per stitch works for me.

ZIGZAG OR OVERLOCK STITCH

I use a wide zigzag or overlock stitch to neaten all my raw edges. This is necessary to prevent fraying at the seams, particularly when you launder your items. If you are layering and quilting a project the seams will all be inside. They will not need overlocking but do make sure that loose threads are clipped off and the back of your work is tidy.

A zigzag stitch may also be used for decorative topstitching, particularly around appliqué shapes. Narrow width and short length zigzag (satin stitch) is a particularly robust edging to appliqués but it takes a lot of practice to get a really neat finish so build up to this!

SEWING SEAMS

Pin the edges together for accuracy but remove the pins as you get to them. For patchwork piecing, use a 0.5cm (¼in) seam allowance. For most other constructions I like to use a 1cm (½in) seam allowance, sometimes trimming back, particularly at corners and on curves, to 3mm (⅛in).

To join strips of fabric with diagonal seams, place the strips at right angles, then sew at a 45-degree angle. Join them with a 0.5cm (¼in) seam allowance and press the seams open.

FUSIBLE APPLIQUÉ

Fusible appliqué is a quick and easy way to embellish all sorts of home-decorating projects, from cushions and throws to bedding, lampshades and bags. You'll need fusible web (see Stockists, page 216). Your appliqués will be the reverse of whatever shape you trace so if you're adding alphabet letters or asymmetric designs make sure the template is reversed.

PREPARING AND FUSING THE APPLIQUÉ

1. Trace around your appliqué shape onto the paper side of the fusible web.

2. Cut the shape out roughly, leave approximately 0.5cm (¼in) all around your traced line.

3. Fuse the roughly cut out shape to the wrong side of your appliqué fabric using an iron. The temperature of the iron will depend on the brand of fusible, so check the manufacturer's instructions. I like to iron through a piece of baking paper to protect my iron from the glue.

4. Cut the appliqué shape out neatly along the drawn line.

5. Remove the paper backing and place the appliqué, glue side down, on the right side of your chosen surface (e.g. your cushion front).

6. Fuse the appliqué to the background fabric with an iron.

FINISHING THE EDGES

Some new fusibles do not need sewing down; the fusible is enough to make it machine washable but most of the time you will want to finish the edges with some kind of topstitching. A small zigzag stitch will do the job nicely, using a matching or toning colour. Every sewing machine is capable of doing this but do take your time, especially around those curves! If your machine has it, try using the blanket stitch on your appliqué edges. This has a charming, 'country' look and adds a very decorative finish. Another easy option is to machine straight stitch just inside the appliqué edge using a matching or toning colour. This is a more casual and modern look very suited to the projects in this book.

MAKING AND APPLYING PIPING

Piping is fabric covered cotton cord applied to the edge of cushions, seat pads and furnishings. It is both decorative and practical as it will make your seams stronger and more resilient. If you're piping a straight line or square then strips cut on the straight of grain will be fine but if you are piping something with curves you will need to cut your strips on the bias so that they will bend.

1. Cut strips to the width needed to cover your cord. I usually work with strips that are 5cm (2in) wide. Join them with diagonal seams and press the seams open.

2. Place the cord onto the wrong side of your fabric strip and fold the strip over it to encase it completely, bringing the raw edges of the fabric strip together. Pin along the strip close to the cord.

3. With the zipper foot on your machine, sew along the strip as close to the cord as you can get.

4. Baste the piping to your chosen fabric, with the piping facing in and all your raw edges aligned. When you turn corners or go around curves you will need to snip into the seam allowances to enable the piping to fit smoothly.

5. Before you sew the piping to your chosen fabric, you will need to join the ends. Unpick a few centimetres (inches) of the machine stitching on your piping at either raw end.

6. Trim the piping cord so that the ends meet and bind them together with thread. Fold under one end of the covering fabric about 1cm (½in) to neaten the edges and slip the other raw end into it.

7. Finally, place your other piece of fabric on top and machine stitch as close to the piping as possible; this will join the two fabrics together with the piping cord neatly sandwiched in the middle. Remove the basting stitches.

MAKING TIES

I use this technique a lot to make ties and tabs. It's a great way to neaten a strip of fabric and it's both accurate and easy.

1. Cut strips of fabric on the lengthwise or crosswise grain to the required width. This should be four times the finished width you require.

2. Fold the strip in half along the length, wrong sides together, and press.

3. Open the strip up and press both the long raw edges in towards the centre crease.

4. Refold along the centre crease to create a tie which is four layers thick and has the long raw edges enclosed.

5. Topstitch along the long folded edge. If you need to neaten the short raw ends just push them inside the tie and topstitch; alternatively fold the short raw end down 1cm (½in) before you stitch.

MITRES

I use mitres on napkins and sometimes on curtains or blinds. They are not hard to do and create a very crisp and neat corner that looks good from every angle.

1. Fold the required hem on two adjacent corners. Press in place.

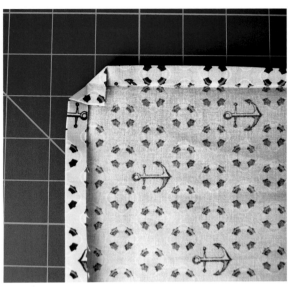

2. Turn in the corner until the pressed lines and the turned-in corner cross. Press in place.

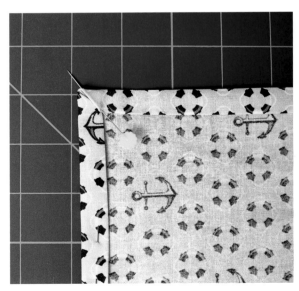

3. Trim away the corner, leaving a 0.5cm (¼in) seam allowance.

4. Fold the side and bottom hem back in place, forming a mitre at the corner.

INSERTING A ZIP

I've always avoided putting zips into projects because I thought they were hard. Trust me, they are not, particularly if you follow this easy method!

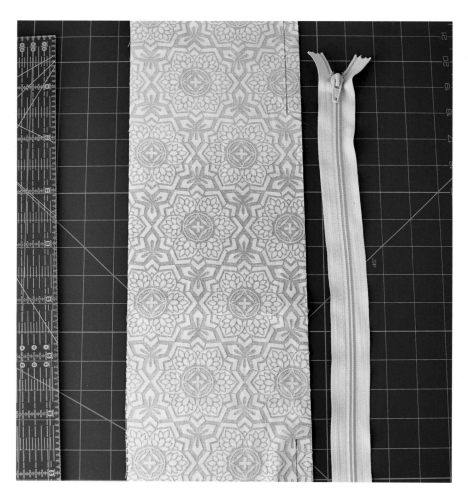

1. Place your two pieces of fabric right sides together and pin and baste with a 1cm (½in) seam allowance. Press the basted seam open.

2. Place your zip over the basted line and mark the beginning and end of the zip (where the teeth start and stop); mark with a pin or a pencil.

3. Take the zip away, refold the fabrics, right sides together and machine sew from the beginning to the first pin (the start of the zip) and backstitch to reinforce the stitching. Then sew from the second pin (the end of the zip) to the end of your fabric. You should have left a gap in the middle where the zip will go. Press the seam open.

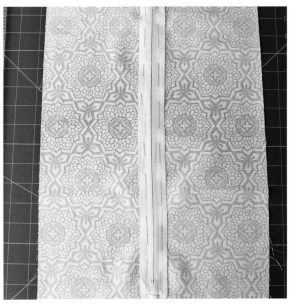

4. Lay your zip down on the back of your fabric, the right side of your zip touching the wrong side of your fabric with the teeth centred on the basted centre. Baste the zip in place.

Working from the right side, sew around the zip with the zipper foot on your machine and sewing approximately 0.5cm (¼in) from the centre seam.

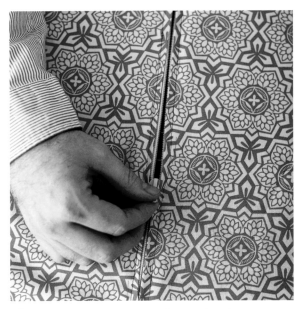

5. Remove all basting stitches and make sure your zip runs smoothly.

LAYERING A QUILT SANDWICH

This is the standard way to put the three layers of a quilt together but it's also a method I regularly use for making quilted cushions, place mats, table runners and the like. The backing and top are layered right sides out and then quilted; this means that the raw edges will need a quilt binding. If you don't want to bind your project use a pieced backing and 'bag out' instead (see page 53). Make sure your quilt backing and wadding are a few inches bigger all round and the quilt top and back are well pressed and wrinkle free before you start.

1. Lay the backing on your work surface, wrong side facing up.

2. Lay the quilt wadding on top and smooth out any wrinkles.

3. Lay the quilt top on top, right side up, and make sure it is straight and smooth.

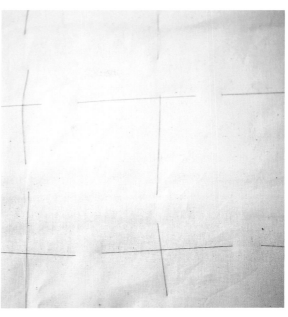

4. Baste the layers together with curved safety pins or hand baste with a needle and thread, taking large stitches through all the layers prior to machine or hand quilting.

OR: I've recently discovered quilt basting spray and I'm a huge fan. Lay the backing down, wrong side up, spray with quilt basting spray then lay the wadding on top, spray again and lay the quilt top on top. The layers are temporarily fused together, ready to machine quilt.

MACHINE SEWN BINDING

Sometimes projects call for a machine sewn bound edge. This is faster than a quilt binding but requires more skill as both sides of the binding are sewn on in one step.

1. Prepare binding strips as if you were making ties (see page 40) but do not stitch. The strips may be cut on the straight of grain or bias, depending on whether the edge you wish to bind is straight or curved.

2. Fold the binding strip over the raw edge of your quilted project and pin in place. Neaten the end by folding one end and slipping the other raw end into it.

3. Topstitch close to the binding edge making certain that you catch the binding on the front and the back at the same time!

MACHINE QUILTING

Use a walking foot for long straight lines and stitching around patches, use a darning foot for free-motion quilting. Use a slightly longer than normal stitch length such as 3.0–3.5mm (⅛in). Make sure the thread ends are finished neatly and trimmed off or buried in the quilt. For large projects consider longarm quilting — you simply send your quilt top away to a professional who will layer and quilt it; all you'll need to do is bind the finished quilt.

BINDING A QUILT

A quilt binding adds a professional, smart and decorative edge to quilts and quilted projects. The technique can also be used to bind any edge and since the two sides of the binding are stitched separately, it's a good choice of binding if your topstitching skills are not 100 per cent perfect.

Once the quilting has been completed you'll need to trim the wadding and backing even with the quilt top. Once this is done you can bind the raw edge.

1. Cut strips of binding fabric, on the straight of grain, 6cm (2½in) wide. Join the strips with diagonal seams until you have enough length to get around the perimeter of your quilted project, plus approximately 10cm (4in) extra.

2. At the start of one short raw edge turn in 1cm (½in) to neaten the end. Start from this neatened edge.

3. Align the raw edges of the binding with the raw edges of the quilt, working on the right side of the quilt. Pin your binding in place.

4. Begin stitching about 10cm (4in) away from the neatened short end and about halfway down one side of your quilt. Use a 0.5cm (¼in) seam allowance to machine stitch the binding to the front of your quilt.

5. When you get 0.5cm (¼in) away from the first corner stop stitching, backstitch for a few stitches and then clip your stitches.

6. Lay your quilt on a flat surface and take the binding strip up until the raw edges of the binding are in line with the quilt edge. Now fold the binding strip back down until the raw edges of the binding and the quilt on the next side are aligned. Pin.

7. Start stitching 0.5cm (¼in) away from the corner and continue sewing to the next corner. Repeat the mitreing process.

8. When you get back to the start, to the neatened short end, just tuck the raw binding edge into the neatened end and finish sewing.

9. The binding is then hand sewn to the back of the quilt.

10. Turn the binding to the back of the quilt and hand sew the folded edge to the back of the quilt with small, neat invisible stitches.

11. When you get to a corner, a neat mitre will form, sew this down securely too.

MAKING A PIECED BACKING

Patterns often call for two shapes to be sewn right sides together with a gap left for turning. Once turned the open edge has to be hand sewn closed. It's often hard to get a really neat finish and you can usually see where the hand sewing has been done. The answer is to make a pieced backing!

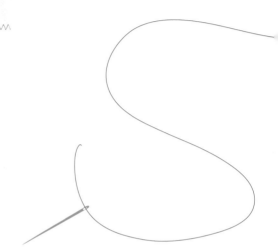

1. Cut the front as normal but for the back you want to cut two pieces of fabric, each one half the size of the front, add an extra 1cm (½in) for joining the two pieces together. Now join the two back panels together, leaving a gap in the middle to allow for turning. If you are using a template to cut the back out (for example the Scented Scrap Heart, page 202) make sure the template is centred over the gap.

2. Sew the two pieces right sides together, all the way round.

3. Turn your work through to the right side through the opening in the back – you will have perfect edges!

4. Hand sew the opening closed.

BAGGING OUT

Bagging out is a similar technique to making a pieced backing, and can be done on small quilts.

1. Lay the wadding down on a flat surface, then the front and the pieced backing of the quilt, right sides together, on top of the wadding.

2. Sew all around the outside edge then turn the quilt through to the right side through the back opening. Press flat then pin or thread baste the quilt.

3. Machine or hand quilt. This type of quilt layer does not require a binding.

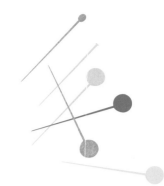

MAKING A
HANGING SLEEVE

*Quilts can be turned into wall art with the addition
of a simple hanging sleeve.*

1. Cut a piece of calico to the width of the quilt and
   32.5cm (13in) deep. Fold the ends in by 2.5cm (1in),
   press and stitch the hem.

2. Fold the calico in half along the length so it is 16cm
   (6½in) wide, right sides together; do not press.
   Sew the long raw edges together with a 1cm (½in)
   seam allowance.

3. Turn through to the right side and centre the long
   seam on the back. Now press the top and bottom
   edges of the sleeve. Slip stitch the sleeve along the
   top and bottom pressed edges to the top/back of
   the quilt you want to hang.

4. Slide a rod or pole through the sleeve to hang
   the quilt.

Stuart's Tip

*If you can, add your hanging sleeve
before you bind the quilt. Align the
top edge of the sleeve with the top
(raw) edge of the quilt and baste.
Now bind your quilt. You will then
only need to hand stitch the bottom
of the sleeve . . . easy!*

EYE MASK

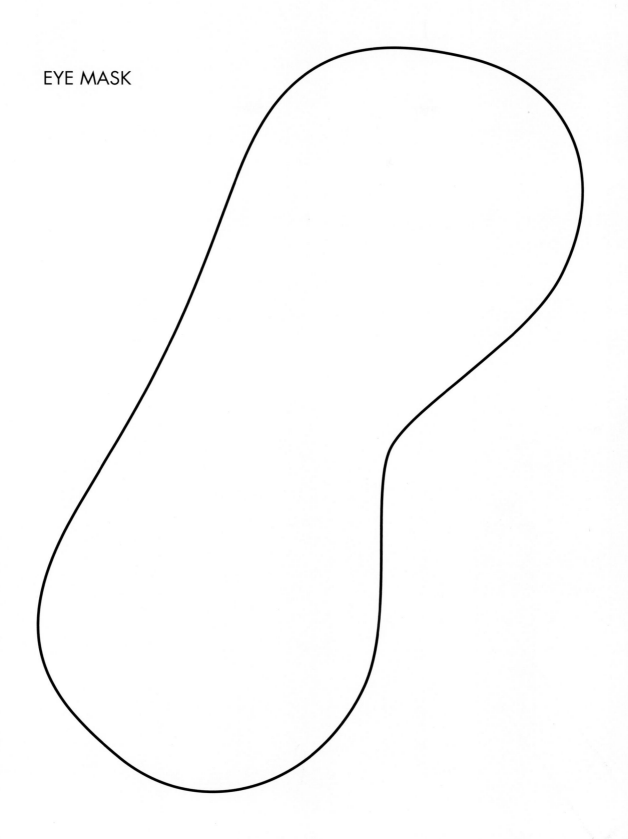

INSPIRED ENTRANCE
NEW ENGLAND

Show visitors your love of all things sewn from the moment they arrive with your fabulous fabric-filled hall. The projects in this chapter combine practical needs for storage with the warming welcome that beautiful textiles alone can provide. Strips and scraps make an easy no sew door wreath and for something a little more challenging tackle my painted floor cloth, an ancient floor covering brought bang up to date with a fresh New England look.

Revamped Picture Frame Noticeboard 64

Seasonal Wreath 66

Painted Floor Cloth 68

Hanging Shoe Tidy 71

Fragrant Coat Hangers 74

REVAMPED PICTURE FRAME NOTICEBOARD

A noticeboard in the hallway is a great way to get your message across, whether it's 'don't forget your keys', 'buy milk' or simply 'I love you!'. The frame gets an easy makeover with scraps of quilt wadding and a smart new fabric cover, which is simply stapled to the back. The glass from the frame is removed and the backboard is given a couple of coats of blackboard paint. Add a little dish nearby to hold chalk for writing those all-important messages.

YOU WILL NEED:
PLAIN PICTURE FRAME
POLYESTER OR COTTON QUILT WADDING THE SIZE OF THE FRAME, PLUS 15CM (6IN) EXTRA ALL ROUND
SPRAY ADHESIVE
STAPLE GUN AND STAPLES
FABRIC THE SIZE OF YOUR FRAME, PLUS 15CM (6IN) EXTRA ALL ROUND
BLACKBOARD PAINT AND PAINTBRUSH

1. Remove the backboard and the glass from the frame. The glass is not needed and can be recycled.

2. Lay the quilt wadding on a large flat surface then lay the frame on top. Cut a piece of wadding approximately 8cm (3in) larger than the frame all round. Cut an 'X' through the wadding in the centre of the frame from corner to corner.

3. Spray the frame with adhesive then lay the wadding on top. Fold the centre of the wadding neatly through to the reverse and staple in place. Trim the excess wadding away. Turn the outer edges of the wadding to the reverse too, staple and trim.

4. Lay your chosen fabric on a flat surface and repeat steps 2 and 3, but this time with the fabric. When you fold the fabric to the back fold under a neat double hem before stapling in place. Make sure the fabric remains wrinkle-free on the front of your frame.

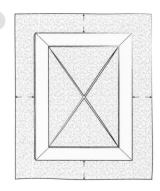

5. Brush any dust off the frame backboard and then apply a coat of blackboard paint. Let it dry and then repeat. If your backboard is in poor condition you might need to cut a new one to size from hardboard.

6. Replace the backboard and clip into place. Your revamped noticeboard is ready to hang. Place some sticks of chalk nearby. Make a hanging heart (see page 202) from matching fabric, and use to wipe your blackboard clean!

**EASY
[NO SEW]**

SEASONAL WREATH

A fabric-trimmed wreath on your front door lets the world know you love material pleasures. This wreath doesn't require any new sewing skills and is so simple you can get the children involved and make one for every season.

YOU WILL NEED:
SCRAPS OF LIGHTWEIGHT COTTON AND LINEN FABRICS
WIRE WREATH FRAME, 30–35CM (12–14IN) IN DIAMETER
RIBBONS AND TRIMMINGS OF YOUR CHOICE
BUTTONS (OPTIONAL)
HOT GLUE GUN (OPTIONAL)

FINISHED SIZE: APPROXIMATELY 38–40CM (15–16IN) IN DIAMETER

1. Cut or tear your fabric into strips that are 2.5x10cm (1x4in). These dimensions are not written in stone and it doesn't matter if your strips vary a bit.

2. Tie each strip of fabric onto the wire wreath frame with a single overhand knot. Keep adding strips of fabric and ribbons or trimmings until the frame is covered.

3. Embellish the wreath with buttons if you wish; just use the hot glue gun to fix them in place.

4. Fix the wreath to your door. I recommend using it on an internal or porch/storm door rather than an external door, as it won't stand up to the elements.

PROJECT VARIATIONS

- *This is a great project for varying throughout the year; just switch up the colours and fabrics used to complement the changing seasons:*

- *Pastels, pale yellow and white for spring or Easter (glue small coloured eggs to the wreath).*

- *Reds, greens and gold for Christmas or a mixture of greens with bright red buttons for holly berries.*

- *Bright pink, teal, purple, orange for a celebration or party wreath.*

PAINTED FLOOR CLOTH

Floor cloths are one of the oldest forms of floor covering and it's not difficult to see why; they can be made to virtually any size or shape and can be painted in any colour or design you like. What's more is they can be easily cleaned with a mop/cloth and warm soapy water. If they get really dirty or scuffed, just remove the varnish and re-do. This project needs to be made over a period of two to three weeks to allow plenty of time for the various layers of gesso, paint and varnish to dry, but the results are well worth the time!

YOU WILL NEED:

8 OR 10OZ CANVAS DUCK, ABOUT 10CM (4IN) BIGGER ON ALL SIDES THAN YOUR FINISHED FLOORCLOTH

TACKS OR A STAPLE GUN

PIECE OF HARDBOARD, ABOUT 15CM (6IN) BIGGER ALL ROUND THAN YOUR FLOORCLOTH

MASKING TAPE

GESSO (OPTIONAL)

PROFESSIONAL ACRYLIC PAINTS, SUCH AS SOFT BODY, IN YOUR CHOICE OF COLOURS

ARTIST'S PROTECTIVE VARNISH

MATTE GEL MEDIUM OR STRONG DOUBLE-SIDED TAPE

FINISHED SIZE: MINE IS 60X127CM (24X50IN) BUT YOU CAN MAKE YOUR FLOOR CLOTH ANY SIZE YOU LIKE; THE ONLY LIMIT IS THE MAXIMUM WIDTH OF YOUR CANVAS.

1. Staple or tack your canvas to the hardboard. Carefully measure out the desired finished size of your floor cloth and mark it on the canvas with a pencil. Apply masking tape around these lines to provide a crisp, neat edge.

2. Most art supplies shops sell canvas duck that has already been primed with gesso. If yours has not been primed, apply one coat of gesso, let dry then sand lightly and repeat. It's a good idea to flip your canvas over and prime the back too, before attaching the hardboard.

3. Once your canvas is primed and dry, paint the whole surface with your chosen background colour. Once this is dry then you are ready to mark out your design. For circles use bowls and plates to lightly mark your design; for stripes mask off lines of unequal widths with masking tape. For a freestyle design, draw with a pencil and let your imagination run wild!

4. Paint your design. For most designs you will need to apply paint, let it dry then re-mask and apply the next colour. Keep your floor cloth in a dust-, pet- and child-free place while you are painting!

5. Once your design is completely finished, let it dry for 48 hours then apply one coat of varnish to isolate your painting. Let this dry then apply a second coat. Two coats of varnish are important because you may get a nasty mark or scuff on your floor cloth that won't clean off with normal detergent. If you do get such a mark, use artist's varnish remover and a lint free cloth to gently remove the top layer of varnish and the mark will disappear with the varnish. Once the floor cloth is clean, you can then re-varnish it.

6. Leave your floor cloth to completely dry, ideally for one to two weeks. Now it's time to turn under the hem. Remove the tacks or staples and trim the cloth to within 2.5cm (1in) of your painted design. Cut a 2.5cm (1in) square out of the hems at each corner then on the back of the floor cloth apply matte gel medium to the hems and fold them down neatly. Apply matte gel medium to the edges as well to really seal the floor cloth. Alternatively you can use strong double-sided tape to fix the hems in place. Leave the hems on the floor cloth to dry for a further 24 hours.

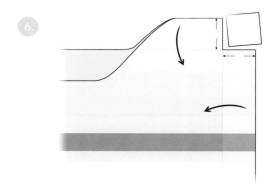

PROJECT VARIATIONS

- *For a different edge treatment, use twill rug binding, which can be ironed in place around the edges of your floor cloth and gives a really neat professional finish.*

- *Prime and apply a base coat to your floor cloth then draw around your children's feet in a 'walking' pattern down the centre of the cloth. Paint the feet, then allow to dry and varnish as before.*

- *Instead of corners, how about curves? Just use a small plate to round off the corners before you edge or bind the floor cloth.*

HANGING SHOE TIDY

This hanging shoe tidy is smart enough to be seen but neat enough to hang on the back of a door and holds up to 12 pairs of shoes. Elasticated top pockets hold footwear snugly and a pleat at the bottom of each pocket means there's plenty of room for even large shoes. Use 1cm (½in) seam allowances throughout.

YOU WILL NEED:

TABS: SIX PIECES DECORATOR WEIGHT FABRIC, EACH 20X20CM (8X8IN)
BACK PANEL: TWO PIECES DECORATOR WEIGHT FABRIC, EACH 72.5X67.5CM (29X27IN)
FRONT PANEL: ONE PIECE DECORATOR WEIGHT FABRIC, 72.5X132.5CM (29X52IN)
QUILT WADDING, 72.5X132.5CM (29X52IN)
POCKET FRONTS: TWELVE PIECES DECORATOR WEIGHT FABRIC, EACH 25X32.5CM (10X13IN)
POCKET BACKS: TWELVE PIECES LINING FABRIC, EACH 25X32.5CM (10X13IN)
APPROXIMATELY 3M (3½YD) ELASTIC, 1CM (½IN) WIDE
SAFETY PIN
AIR-ERASABLE MARKING PEN
DOWEL ROD, 70X2CM (27½X¾IN), PLUS TWO SMALL FINIALS (NO BIGGER THAN 2CM/¾IN WIDE)
180CM (72IN) DECORATIVE CORD TO HANG THE SHOE TIDY
TWO DECORATIVE TASSELS (OPTIONAL)

FINISHED SIZE: 70X130CM (27½X51IN), EXCLUDING HANGING TABS

1.   To make the hanging tabs take two of the 20cm (8in) squares of fabric and, with right sides together, stitch together along two opposite sides. Turn the tabs through to the right side and press flat, then press the tabs in half. Repeat with the other four squares to make three tabs in total.

2.   With right sides together, sew the two 72.5x67.5cm (29x27in) pieces for the back together along one of the longer sides, leaving a gap in the middle approximately 25cm (10in) wide for turning through. Press the seam allowance open.

3. Lay the 72.5x132.5cm (29x52in) front panel right side up on a clean flat surface. Position the tabs at the top of the panel, one in the centre and the remaining two 2.5cm (1in) from either side. The raw edges of the tabs should be level with the raw edge of the front panel. Now place the quilt wadding on top and finally the pieced-together back, with the gap running down the centre of your shoe tidy, right side facing down. Pin all around the outer edges.

4. Sew all around the perimeter of the shoe tidy using a 1cm (½in) seam allowance. Trim the corners to reduce the bulk then turn through to the right side through the opening in the back. Press the outer edges, folding the hanging tabs up and away from the shoe tidy. Topstitch around the shoe tidy, 0.5cm (¼in) from the outer edge.

5. Make the pockets. With right sides together, stitch one pocket front to one pocket back along the top edge, flip the top fabric back so the right side is facing out and press. Stitch a channel along the top, 2cm (¾in) from the stitched edge for the elastic casing.

6. Attach a safety pin to the end of your elastic and feed it through the channel. Remove the pin then draw the elastic back until it is 2.5cm (1in) from the pocket edge and stitch firmly in place. Pull the elastic back until the top of the pocket measures 18cm (7in) and again stitch the elastic firmly in place. The top of the pocket should measure 18cm (7in) gathered up and the elastic should be stitched in place 2.5cm (1in) in from either side.

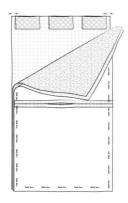 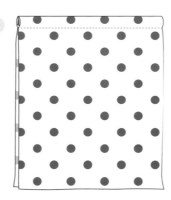 

7. Fold the sides of the pocket in by 1cm (½in) and press. Unfold and then overlock or zigzag the raw edges. Make a 5cm (2in) pleat in the centre of each pocket and baste, overlock or zigzag the bottom raw edge, then fold under a 1cm (½in) hem. Refold the side hems. Repeat steps 5–7 to make twelve pockets in total.

8. Attach the pockets to the shoe tidy. Measure and mark a line with an air-erasable marking pen across the shoe tidy, 15cm (6in) down from the top edge (the one with the tabs). Position three pockets across this mark, lining up the top of your pockets with the line. Pin in place then topstitch around each pocket, close to the edges. Measure and mark a line 10cm (4in) down from the bottom of this first row of pockets and add another row of pockets.

9. Repeat step 8 to attach all 12 pockets. There should be 5cm (2in) left at the bottom of your shoe tidy.

10. Attach the finials to either end of the dowel then thread the dowel rod through the hanging tabs. Tie the cord at the finial ends, adding tassels if you wish.

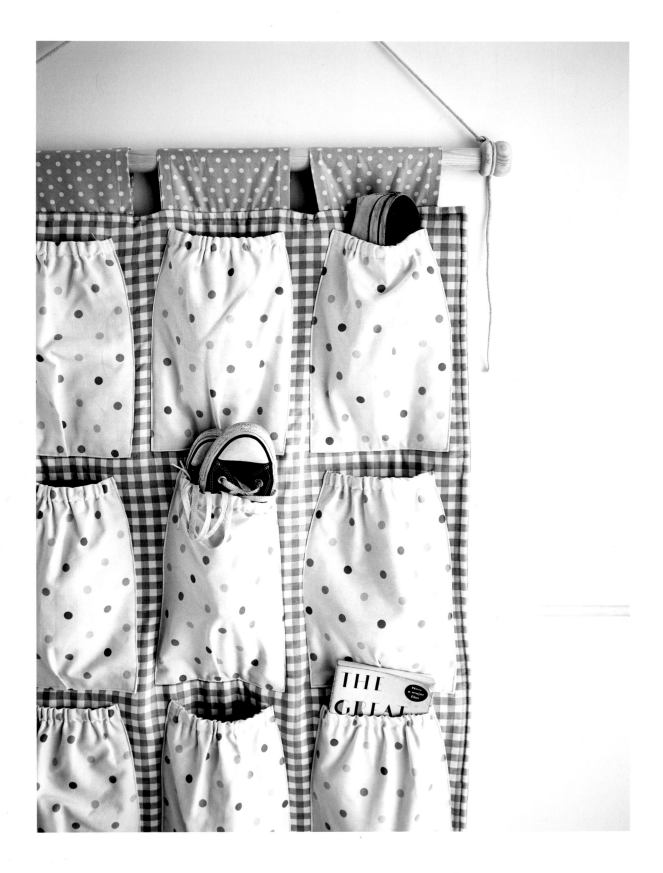

FRAGRANT COAT HANGERS

Keep a few of these padded and covered coat hangers in your downstairs cloakroom and store your guests' outerwear in scented style. The hangers themselves are gently padded to help prevent delicate clothes and knitwear stretching at the shoulders and each has a fragrant heart shaped sachet to impart a rich and exotic scent.

YOU WILL NEED:
SCRAPS OF QUILT WADDING
FABRIC GLUE OR QUILT BASTING SPRAY, SUCH AS 505
WOODEN BOOMERANG-STYLE COAT HANGER (I.E. ONE WITHOUT A TROUSER BAR)
23CM (9IN) MEDIUM-WEIGHT COTTON OR HOME DECORATING WEIGHT FABRIC
MATCHING THREAD
90CM (35½IN) MATCHING FINE RIBBON, APPROXIMATELY 3MM (⅛IN) WIDE
SMALL SCRAP OF COORDINATING FABRIC FOR THE HEART, APPROXIMATELY 9X18CM (3½X7IN)
½ TSP MIXED SPICE
½ TSP GROUND CLOVES
HEART TEMPLATE (SEE PAGE 59), CUT OUT OF TISSUE PAPER
SCISSORS OR PINKING SHEARS

1. Cut your wadding scraps into strips approximately 4cm (1½in) wide. Spray lightly with quilt basting spray and then wind the strips around the wooden part of the coat hanger to cover it neatly.

2. Fold your fabric in half, right sides together, then place your padded coat hanger on top of the fabric so that a little over half of the hanger (one side) is on top of the fabric. Draw around that half of the hanger adding a 1cm (½in) seam allowance all round. Extend the lines by about 1cm (½in) over the midpoint.

3. Cut out along the lines then use this as a template to cut another two pieces of fabric to fit the other side of the hanger. Take one fabric pair and sew all around the long sides, leaving the short side open for turning. Repeat with the other pair, turn both right sides out and press.

4. Slip each half onto the padded coat hanger. There should be about 1cm (½in) overlap in the middle; turn this raw edge in by 1cm (½in) then stitch the opening closed using a slip stitch or ladder stitch.

5. Use about 45cm (18in) of the fine ribbon to cover the join then wind it around the wire part of the hanger once or twice, finally tying a neat bow. Trim the ends of the ribbon if you like.

6. To make the scented heart sachets, cut your pretty fabric scrap in half to make two 9cm (3½in) squares. Lay one down, wrong side up, and place a similar sized scrap of quilt wadding on top. Next spoon the mixed spices and ground cloves into the centre, followed by more wadding, and finally the other square of fabric on top, right side up.

7. Place the heart template on top of the sandwich and pin through all the layers. Carefully sew around the heart with a small stitch on your sewing machine. Trim around the heart, leaving about 0.5cm (¼in) of fabric outside the stitching – use pinking shears if you have them.

8. Fold the remaining fine ribbon in half and knot the folded end. Place the knotted end of the ribbon at the top of the heart and sew back and forth over the knot a few times to secure the ribbon to the heart. Tie the scented heart sachet to the wire part of the coat hanger.

Stuart's Tip

See page 202 for a photo of the finished scented heart. Individually, they make lovely gifts too!

LIBERATED LOUNGING

MODERN BRIGHTS

Ahh the lounge — the clue is in the name — l-o-u-n-g-e.
A place to lay, to sprawl, to relax. A comfy sofa or chair needs some
beautiful cushions and bolsters to add to the plump splendour and
encourage decadent reclining. Simple lined curtains add lots of style
and a throw in a really smart fabric can add luxury, warmth and
sophistication to any type of seating.

Simple Piped Cushion 80

Patchwork Cushion 82

Simple Lined Curtains with Pencil Pleat Heading 84

Bolster Cushion 87

Sofa Throw 90

SIMPLE PIPED CUSHION

This is a very easy, smart and versatile cushion. It has optional piping and covered button detail and would look great in any fabric! The button, which is covered in a contrast fabric, will need removing and the edge unpicking for laundering.

YOU WILL NEED:
45CM (18IN) FABRIC FOR THE CUSHION FRONT AND BACK
11CM (4½ IN) CONTRAST FABRIC FOR THE PIPING (OPTIONAL)
1.8M (2YD) PIPING CORD (OPTIONAL)
40X40CM (16X16IN) CUSHION PAD
ONE BUTTON, 4CM (1½IN) IN DIAMETER
MATCHING FABRIC FOR THE BUTTON
ONE MATCHING BUTTON, 2CM (¾IN) IN DIAMETER
DOLL NEEDLE

FINISHED SIZE: 40X40CM (16X16IN)

1. Cut two 43cm (17in) squares of fabric: one for the front, one for the back. You could use contrasting fabrics if you wish.

2. If you are adding piping, cut two strips of contrast fabric to cover the cord, each 5cm (2in) by the width of the fabric. Join these end to end with diagonal seams and cover the piping cord (see Making and Applying Piping, page 37).

3. With right side up, pin and baste the piping to the outer edges of the cushion front panel, keeping the raw edges even. You'll need to snip into the seam allowance on the piping at the corners so that it bends. Join the ends of the piping following the instructions on page 38, then machine stitch the piping in place.

4. Pin the cushion back to the cushion front, right sides together, and sew around all sides, leaving a 25cm (10in) gap for inserting the cushion pad. Snip off the corners to reduce the bulk and turn the cushion cover through to the right side. Insert the cushion pad and sew the gap closed with invisible hand stitches.

5. Cover the 4cm (1½in) button with fabric. This is done simply by cutting a circle approximately 1cm (½in) bigger all round, gathering the outer edge by hand and pulling up over the button, but check the manufacturer's instructions as they can vary.

6. Using a doll needle, sew the covered button to the centre of the cushion front, passing the needle right through the cushion pad and sewing the smaller button to the cushion back.

MEDIUM

PATCHWORK CUSHION

Very basic patchwork transforms this simple cushion into something much more stylish and you can see from my examples in the lounge and hallway how changing the placement of the colours makes a huge difference. The piping and covered buttons are optional but add a lot of impact and are worth the extra time! Use 1cm (½in) seam allowances throughout.

YOU WILL NEED:
SIXTEEN 11CM (4½IN) SQUARES ASSORTED FABRICS FOR THE PATCHWORK
11CM (4½IN) CONTRAST FABRIC FOR THE PIPING
1.8M (2YD) PIPING CORD
43CM (17IN) SQUARE FABRIC FOR THE CUSHION BACKING
40X40CM (16X16IN) CUSHION PAD
NINE 2CM (¾IN) COVERED BUTTONS FOR THE CUSHION FRONT
NINE SMALL BUTTONS FOR THE CUSHION BACK
DOLL NEEDLE

FINISHED SIZE: 40X40CM (16X16IN)

1. Arrange the sixteen squares into four rows of four until you are pleased
    with the arrangement. Sew the pieces of each row together, pressing
    the seam allowances to the right on rows one and three and to the
    left on rows two and four. Then sew the rows together, locking the
    seam allowances together. Your finished patchwork square should be
    41.5x41.5cm (16½x16½in).

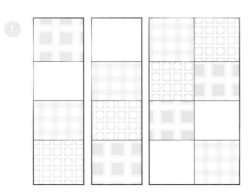

2. Cut two strips of contrast fabric to cover the piping cord, each 5cm (2in) wide by the width of the fabric and join them end to end with diagonal seams. Use to cover the piping cord (see Making and Applying Piping, page 37).

3. Continue to make up the cushion by sewing on the piping, adding the backing, turning through and inserting the cushion pad (see the instructions for the Simple Piped Cushion, page 80). Sew the opening closed.

4. Make five–nine covered buttons in colours to complement your patchwork (see step 5 of the Simple Piped Cushion, page 80). Sew them onto the front of your cushion at the patchwork intersections. Use a doll needle to go right through the cushion, picking up a small button on the back of the cushion.

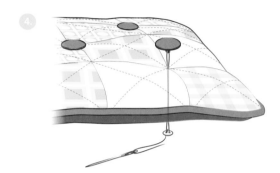

MEDIUM

SIMPLE LINED CURTAINS
WITH PENCIL PLEAT HEADING

Lined curtains can cost a small fortune to have made to measure and buying ready-made often involves compromising on the fit, colour or fabric. Remember the adage here: measure twice and cut once – never was this truer than when you are making curtains. Make sure all your measurements are accurate before you start cutting and your curtains will hang straight and true!

YOU WILL NEED:
MAIN FABRIC OF YOUR CHOICE (SEE ESTIMATING FABRIC BOX FOR DIMENSIONS)
LINING FABRIC
PENCIL PLEAT HEADING TAPE, FOUR TIMES THE WIDTH OF CURTAIN POLE PLUS 25CM (10IN)

1. Join widths of main fabric together to get to your required width, taking into account any pattern that needs to be matched up, then cut your curtain panels. Repeat for the lining but cut the lining fabric 10cm (4in) narrower than the main fabric. Mark the centre of both the main fabric and the lining fabric at the top and bottom with a small notch cut into the fabric.

2. Place the main fabric and lining fabric right sides together; remember that the main fabric is wider than the lining. Pin and sew one side hem with a 1cm (½in) seam allowance, then match up the other side hem, pin and sew. Turn the curtain through to the right side and match the centre notches. Because the main fabric is wider, the main fabric will turn to the lining at the side seams. Press these side seams carefully.

ESTIMATING FABRIC

- *For the width measure the width of your curtain pole and multiply by two, then add 15cm (6in) to this width to allow for the centre overlap.*

- *For the length measure the length from the bottom of your curtain rings to the floor and add 20cm (8in) to this length for the hems.*

- *Each curtain will need to be made to these dimensions and, generally speaking, you will be making two curtains for each window. You'll need extra fabric if there is a pattern to match as you will be joining widths of fabric together.*

- *Buy the same amount of lining fabric, less any extra allowed for pattern matching.*

3. Turn up the bottom hem, main fabric and lining together, first by 5cm (2in), then again by 10cm (4in). Pin and then sew the bottom hem.

4. Turn the top hem down by 5cm (2in) and press. Place the heading tape across the back of the curtain about 1cm (½in) down from the top edge. Free the heading tape cords at either end and tie them loosely together, then turn under the raw edge of the heading tape at either end and stitch. Pin the heading tape in place then stitch all along the long edges of the heading tape.

5. Pull the cords to gather up the heading tape to the required curtain width. One end of the cords are neatly knotted and the other end, where you pulled all the cords to gather, will need winding up into a bundle and tucking under the folded end of the heading tape.

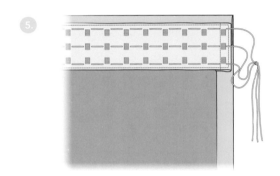

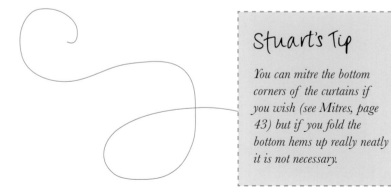

Stuart's Tip

You can mitre the bottom corners of the curtains if you wish (see Mitres, page 43) but if you fold the bottom hems up really neatly it is not necessary.

BOLSTER CUSHION

I love bolster cushions – they work in so many rooms. They're great on the bed as a neck roll, in the garden to add comfort to sunbathing, and in the lounge they make seating look significantly smarter. This cushion has piped edges and a neat zip and adds a sleek and sophisticated look to either end of any sofa. Use 1cm (½in) seam allowances throughout.

YOU WILL NEED:
45CM (18IN) FABRIC FOR THE BOLSTER COVER
DRESSMAKER'S TISSUE PAPER
11CM (4½IN) CONTRAST OR MATCHING FABRIC TO COVER THE PIPING CORD
MATCHING SEWING THREAD
150CM (60IN) PIPING CORD
30CM (12IN) ZIP
BOLSTER CUSHION PAD 45X23CM (18X9IN) – I LOVE FEATHER-FILLED CUSHION PADS

FINISHED SIZE: 45X23CM·(18X9IN)

1. From the main fabric cut a panel that is 65x48cm (26x19in). Then cut two 25cm (10in) diameter circles for the bolster ends. If your bolster ends are not the correct size then you can use dressmaker's tissue paper to create templates.

2. From the fabric for the piping, cut enough 5cm (2in) strips on the bias to cover 150cm (60in) of piping cord. Join the strips and cover the piping cord (see Making and Applying Piping, page 37). Clip into the seam allowance of the piping cord at regular intervals so it is easier to shape.

3. Take the main fabric panel, fold it in half, right sides together and long edge to long edge. Sew along the 48cm (19in) side with long basting stitches and a 1cm (½in) seam allowance.

4. Press the seam open then re-fold it and machine stitch (with a regular stitch length this time) the first and last 9cm (3½in), leaving a 30cm (12in) gap in the centre. Remove the basting stitches and centre the zip over the gap. Baste the zip in position and then topstitch into place (see Inserting a Zip, page 44). Undo the zip.

5. Cut the piping into two equal lengths and baste around both circular end pieces, joining the ends neatly (see Making and Applying Piping, page 37). With right sides together, pin the piped end pieces to the ends of the main panel. Using a piping foot or zipper foot on your machine, sew the bolster ends onto the main panel as close to the piping as you can get. Clip seam allowances where necessary to get a smooth curve.

6. Turn the bolster cover through to the right side and insert the bolster pad. Close the zip.

PROJECT VARIATIONS

- *Add a covered button or tassel to either end of the bolster.*

- *For a patchwork version, make the main panel from a series of strips, pieced together to form a panel of 65x48cm (26x19in).*

SOFA THROW

Give sofas an instant update with a beautiful sofa throw. Use a richly patterned or plain double-sided fabric so the throw will look equally stylish from either side. Add a wide contrast or toning border and tassels for a bit of extra class.

YOU WILL NEED:
1.8M (2YD) MAIN FABRIC (WOOL OR CHENILLE WORK WELL), 150CM (60IN) WIDE
1.8M (2YD) CONTRAST FABRIC FOR BINDING THE EDGES
MATCHING SEWING THREAD
FOUR TASSELS (OPTIONAL)

FINISHED SIZE: 150X175CM (60X70IN)

1. Cut a panel from your main fabric 150x175cm (60x70in).

2. From your contrast fabric cut four strips of fabric: two that are 150x20cm (60x8in) and two that are 180x20cm (71x8in) wide.

3. Fold each binding strip in half along the long side and press, then fold in a 2.5cm (1in) hem in along each long side.

4. Apply the 150cm (60in) binding strips first. Cover the raw edges of the main panel, pin and topstitch in place.

5. Fold in 2.5cm (1in) hems at either short end of the long binding strips to neaten. Apply to the long sides of the main panel, pin then topstitch in place, catching both sides.

6. Sew the tassels, if using, to each corner by hand.

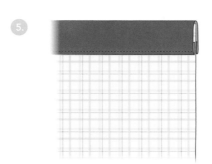

PROJECT VARIATION

If your chosen fabric is one-sided, you can cut a backing fabric to the same size, spray lightly with quilt basting spray and fuse the layers, wrong sides together. Bind as above then add some evenly-spaced buttons through both layers to hold them together.

RUSTIC KITCHEN
TRADITIONAL COUNTRY

I've never been one to run screaming from a cliché and I won't back down now. The kitchen really is the heart of any home – there, I said it! It's where many of us spend a large chunk of our waking hours when we are at home. We cook, we eat, we entertain, we supervise homework, we mend broken hearts over a glass of rosé (just me? Surely not?). But take out the fabric and the smell of baking bread and most of us are left with a very stark, often white, glossy, hard room. Not much heart there if the softness is removed, making this a room that simply cries out for a fabric makeover! Everything in a kitchen takes quite a battering so make sure your seams are well stitched and secure, and your chosen fabrics are easy to launder.

For this country-style kitchen I chose rich shades of terracotta, leaf green and navy in modern, graphic prints, with some cream and tan thrown in to lighten the look. It's practical, warm and easy to live with.

Eco Shopping Tote Bag 96

Everyday Napkins 99

Hot Pads 101

Revampled Kitchen Towels and Drying Cloths 104

Cook's Apron 106

Child's Apron 108

Kitchen Seat Cushions 112

Café Curtain 115

Everyday Place Mats 118

ECO SHOPPING TOTE BAG

Let's rid the world of plastic bags, one gorgeous Eco Shopping Tote Bag at a time. This bag is easy, fast and sturdy. Here's an idea: don't make one bag, make two and take them both to the supermarket the next time you shop. Use one and give one to the person in front of you. Don't forget to tell them where to find the pattern!

YOU WILL NEED:
45CM (18IN) OUTER FABRIC (MINIMUM 105CM/42IN USABLE WIDTH)
45CM (18IN) LINING FABRIC
45CM (18IN) MEDIUM-WEIGHT IRON-ON INTERFACING
MATCHING SEWING THREAD
FINISHED SIZE: 40½X40½CM (16X16IN), PLUS SHOULDER STRAP

1. Cut out two pieces from the outer fabric, each 43x43cm (17x17in). Do the same with the lining fabric so you have four pieces in total. Cut out one shoulder strap pieces from the outer fabric that is 10x90cm (4x36in). Apply interfacing to the two lining pieces and the shoulder strap.

2. Fold the shoulder strip in half lengthwise, wrong sides together and press. Fold both raw edges under by about 0.5cm (¼in) and press, then topstitch down both long edges, 3mm (⅛in) in from the edges to make a sturdy shoulder strap.

3. Place the two outer fabric squares right sides together and sew around both sides and the bottom. Bring the side and bottom seam allowance together on one side and press flat. Measure 4cm (1½in) in from the corner and mark a diagonal line, 'cutting off' the corner. Sew along this line then cut the corner off, leaving a 1cm (½in) seam allowance to 'bag' the corner. Do the same on the other corner. Make the bag lining in exactly the same way using the lining squares but leave a gap of 15cm (6in) wide in the middle of the bottom edge seam for turning.

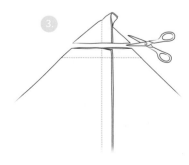

4. Turn the outer bag right sides out and pin the shoulder strap in place on the side seams with the raw edges meeting and the strap hanging under the bag. Now place the outer bag and pinned strap inside the bag lining, right sides together. Align the top raw edges and pin all round the top.

5. Sew around the bag top with a 2.5cm (1in) seam allowance. Reinforce the seam where the shoulder strap joins by going over the stitching line a couple of times.

6. Turn the bag through to the right side through the opening in the lining. Turn the shoulder strap up and press, then topstitch around the top edge of the tote bag, 1cm (½in) from the top of the bag. You could reinforce the shoulder strap attachment by sewing a rectangle over where it joins the bag if you wish. Do this on both sides.

7. Slip stitch the gap in the lining closed.

PROJECT VARIATIONS

- *Add a simple patch pocket to one of the lining squares before you make up the lining bag – useful for keeping your purse, keys or mobile phone handy.*

- *If you prefer short handles, cut two 10x43cm (4x17in) strips, fold and press them as two separate pieces, topstitch as before and then join them to the front and back of the bag.*

- *Use thermal insulating wadding instead of interfacing. This makes a nice sturdy bag and has the added advantage that it will keep frozen and chilled food colder for longer! Thermal insulating wadding can be a bit slippery so pin the layers together really well or use quilt basting spray (see page 47) to hold the wadding to the wrong side of the lining while you are constructing your eco bag.*

- *Add braid, fusible appliqués or fancy buttons to the front of your bag. Make each one unique.*

- *Get the children involved! Make the shopping tote in 8oz cotton duck canvas then let the children decorate the outside of the bag with fabric paints or fabric markers. Add beads, buttons or sequins. You could scale the pattern down to make a smaller bag – then the children can help carry the shopping too!*

EVERYDAY NAPKINS

These easy napkins are fast to make, coordinate beautifully with the place mats on page 118 and will keep fingers and clothes clean during mealtimes. Contrast or coordinate with your crockery or make seasonal sets to change throughout the year! Smaller than the dining room napkins and single-sided, they are perfect for everyday use and regular laundering. Use six different but coordinating fabrics to make a set of napkins.

YOU WILL NEED (FOR ONE NAPKIN):
45CM (18IN) SQUARE OF FABRIC (TRY QUILTING SHOPS FOR 'FAT QUARTERS')
MATCHING SEWING THREAD

FINISHED SIZE: 40X40CM (16X16IN)

1. Turn a double 1cm (½in) hem on all four sides, mitreing the corners as you go (see Mitres, page 43).

2. Topstitch the hem in place with matching sewing thread.

Stuart's Tip

For more dressed-up napkins, see how to make the Napkins for all Seasons, page 130.

PROJECT VARIATIONS

- *Theme your napkins to complement your meal: use intense spice colours (paprika, chilli pepper, turmeric and clove) for Indian meals, capsicum/bell pepper reds, yellows and greens for Mexican and rich purples, teals and gold for Chinese.*

- *Look for themed fabrics – you'll find there's pretty much every option available online – balloons, chilli peppers, world maps . . . the possibilities are almost endless!*

HOT PADS

These hot pads can be whipped up in no time and are so fun and useful you'll want to make them for every season. I like to make my hot pads in pairs for lifting things like casserole dishes out of the oven. By using insulated quilt wadding in the centre, your hot pads are functional as well as stylish.

YOU WILL NEED:
TWO 20CM (8IN) SQUARES OF FABRIC FOR THE HOT PAD TOPS
AIR-ERASABLE MARKING PEN
TWO 20CM (8IN) SQUARES FOR THE HOT PAD BACKS
TWO 20CM (8IN) SQUARES OF THERMAL INSULATED QUILT WADDING
MATCHING SEWING THREAD
11CM (4½IN) FABRIC FOR THE BINDING AND HANGING LOOP

FINISHED SIZE: MAKES TWO PADS, 20X20CM (8X8IN)

1. Mark vertical and horizontal straight lines on the right side of your top fabric, 2.5cm (1in) apart; these are the quilting lines. Alternatively you could sew lines in one direction only, as I have. I like to vary the quilting lines depending on the design of the fabric I'm using. Be experimental; a small item like this is a great opportunity for practice!

2. Lay the backing square down, wrong side up, place the thermal insulated wadding on top, then the marked top fabric, right side facing up. Pin the layers together.

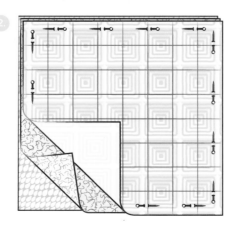

3. Using the walking foot on your machine, quilt along the marked lines, removing the pins as you go.

4. Cut one strip of binding fabric, 5cm (2in) wide by Width of Fabric (WOF). This length will be slightly longer than you need, you can trim it down when you make the hanging loop. Press the fabric in half along the long edge then press the raw edges into the centre fold to create the binding.

5. Starting at one corner, fold the binding over the raw hot pad edge and pin in place. Carefully topstitch close to the edge of the binding, catching the top and bottom at the same time. When you get to within 1cm (½in) of each corner, carefully fold a mitre then continue sewing (see Mitres, page 43).

6. When you get back to the start sew right off the end of the hot pad, continue along the binding only to sew the folded edges together for about 15cm (6in). Neaten the short raw edge too by folding it over twice. Fold the length of unattached binding back to create a hanging loop and stitch it securely to the hot pad.

7. Repeat the steps to make another hot pad to match.

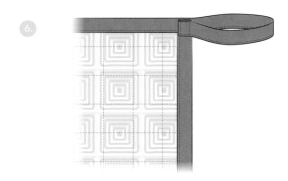

PROJECT VARIATIONS

• *To make a trivet/mat for placing hot pans or casserole dishes on a work surface or table, simply increase the size of the hot pad to 25x25cm (10x10in). You will need two strips for your binding joined end to end. I think it's a good idea to still make the loop so that you can hang your trivet when not in use.*

• *Instead of straight corners you could round the corners by drawing around a saucer or small plate after quilting. Cut the excess off and bind the edges. As the edge is curved you will need to cut your binding from bias strips of fabric, still cut 5cm (2in) wide.*

REVAMPED KITCHEN TOWELS
AND DRYING CLOTHS

A kitchen towel or drying cloth gets a quick and easy makeover with fabric scraps. It's a super easy way to create a unified look in your kitchen and makes drying the dishes just a little more stylish!

YOU WILL NEED:

FABRIC SCRAPS
MATCHING SEWING THREAD
PLAIN KITCHEN TOWEL OR DRYING CLOTH
STRIP OF PLAIN FACING FABRIC (SEE STEP 2)
COORDINATING RIBBON, TWICE THE WIDTH OF YOUR TOWEL PLUS
A COUPLE OF INCHES (OPTIONAL)

1. Cut the fabric scraps into strips between 2.5–5cm (1–2in) wide and about 15cm (6in) long. Sew these scraps together to make a pieced band that is about 2.5cm (1in) wider than your towel.

2. Cut the pieced band to 12.5cm (5in) by the width of your towel, plus an extra 2.5cm (1in) for the hems. Cut a piece of facing fabric to the same size and place it right sides together with the pieced band. Sew both long edges together and then turn the faced strip through to the right side.

3. Turn under a 1cm (½in) hem at each short end and pin to the right side of your towel, over the woven band. If your towel doesn't have a woven band, position the faced strip about 5–8cm (2–3in) up from the lower edge. Pin in place.

4. Pin the ribbon, if using, to the top and bottom of the band, neatening the raw short edge. Topstitch around the outer edge and along the inner long edge of each ribbon to secure the band to the towel.

PROJECT VARIATIONS

- *Add ric rac or braid to either or both edges of the faced band.*

- *Use scraps of fabric left over from the other kitchen sewing projects to create a unified look.*

COOK'S APRON

As soon as the weather warms up I'm out in the garden with the barbecue fired up. More often than not I can't wait for good weather and brave the cold just to smell and taste food cooking over hot coals. A sturdy apron is an essential piece of kit for any man cooking in the garden; it protects clothes and exposed flesh from splashes but more importantly it defines you as Head Chef!

YOU WILL NEED:

PATTERN PIECES A (MAIN BODY) AND B (POCKET) (SEE PAGE 56)

120CM (48IN) MEDIUM-/HEAVYWEIGHT CANVAS, COTTON DRILL OR CALICO

ROTARY CUTTING EQUIPMENT (SEE PAGE 27)

MATCHING SEWING THREAD

FINISHED SIZE: TO FIT MOST ADULTS

1. First cut out pattern pieces A and B from your fabric. Mark out the pocket, neck strap and waist tie position on the main body.

2. Using a rotary cutter and the remnants of fabric, cut out the neck strap, which is 60cm (24in) long by 8cm (3in) wide. Then cut out the two waist ties, which are 92.5cm (37in) long by 8cm (3in) wide (see Making Ties, page 40).

3. Fold the neck strap in half along its long edge and press. Open the strip out, fold under the raw edges on each side by 1cm (½in) and press. Refold the strip to form a neatened strap that is now 2.5cm (1in) wide. Topstitch close to the open edge. Do the same with both waist ties but also turn in one short end by 1cm (½in) twice to form a neat end. Again, topstitch to close and neaten.

4. Make the pocket. Fold the top edge down by 1cm (½in) and press. Repeat to make a double hem and topstitch close to the edge. Now fold in the side and bottom hems by 1cm (½in) but press only – do not stitch yet. Fold the pocket in half and crease the centre lightly to mark the pocket division. Pin the pocket to the apron front using the placement markings, then pin and topstitch around the sides and bottom to attach the pocket. Reinforce the pocket corners by stitching a small triangle. Sew a couple of lines down the centre of the pocket to divide it into two.

5. Hem the edge of the apron. Start with the curved hems; you may need to clip into the hem allowance a little to create a smooth hem. Fold under a neat 1cm (½in) hem and press. Repeat to enclose the raw edges and then topstitch the hem.

6. Next fold under a double 2cm (¾in) hem on the top neck edge. Tuck the raw edges of the neck strap under this hem at the marked points, with the neck strap hanging down, then topstitch across the entire neck edge hem. Now turn the neck strap up into its final position and stitch the neck strap into position by stitching a rectangle.

7. For the side hems turn under a double 1cm (½in) hem, tuck the raw ends of the waist ties in at the marked points, stitch the hem then fold the ties out and stitch again.

8. Finally turn under a double 1cm (½in) for the bottom hem and topstitch in place.

9. Get the barbecue lit, it's time to cook!

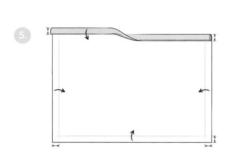

PROJECT VARIATIONS

- *The apron can be shortened (take a few cm/inches off the bottom edge) or narrowed (fold the pattern in half lengthwise, cut down this line and overlap the pattern pieces).*

- *Change the pocket shape, curve the lower edge or make two smaller patch pockets.*

- *Use a contrast fabric for the pocket, neck strap and waist ties.*

- *Embellish the pocket and hems with ric rac braid.*

- *Personalise the apron with a name or appliquéd motifs.*

MEDIUM

CHILD'S APRON

Children love to cook and help out in the kitchen! My mum had me peeling veg and potatoes and making cakes from about the age of six or seven. I learned kitchen craft and a love of cooking from her, she also taught me to make the best gravy in the world. No kitchen helper is complete without his or her own pint-sized apron and this one even has a 'wooden spoon' appliquéd into the pocket! Adding the appliqué makes this apron a little harder than the regular adult size but it's so cute I think it's worth the extra effort.

YOU WILL NEED:
45CM (18IN) MAIN FABRIC
PATTERN PIECES A (MAIN BODY) AND B (WOODEN SPOON) (SEE PAGES 56 AND 58)
MATCHING SEWING THREAD
SCRAP OF BROWN FABRIC FOR THE WOODEN SPOON
FUSIBLE WEB
25X25CM (10X10IN) SQUARE SCRAP OF FABRIC FOR THE POCKET

FINISHED SIZE: TO FIT AN AVERAGE NINE-YEAR-OLD

1. Fold your main fabric in half, right sides together and place pattern piece A on top, with the fold and the centre of the apron aligned. Pin in place and then cut out. Transfer the pocket, neck strap and waist tie position markings.

2. Cut three strips of fabric from the remainder of the main fabric, each 8x50cm (3x20in). Two of them are for the waist ties and the remaining one is for the neck strap. Fold and press these strips in half along the long edges, then fold the raw edges in to meet the centre fold. Neaten one end of each waist tie by turning the short raw edge as well. Press and topstitch along the tucked-in short edge and down one side to make three strips that are approximately 50x2cm (20x¾in).

3. Use pattern piece B to cut one wooden spoon out of brown fabric. Using the fusible web, fuse it to the front of the apron (see Fusible Appliqué, page 34) and topstitch in place.

4. Cut a pocket that is 25x22cm (10x8½in). Fold under 1cm (½in) hems at the shorter sides and the longer bottom edge and then turn under a double 1cm (½in) hem in along the top edge. Topstitch this top double hem in matching sewing thread. Position the pocket on the apron front, covering the lower edge of the appliquéd spoon. Pin in place then topstitch the pocket in place, reinforcing the corners.

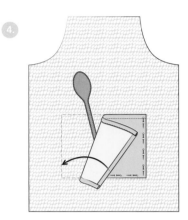

5. Make double 0.5cm (¼in) hems at each curved armhole edge and stitch in place. Fold a double 1cm (½in) hem at the top (neck) edge and tuck the raw edges of the neck strap under this hem. Pin, then topstitch across the entire neck edge hem. Now turn the neck strap up into its final position and reinforce the neck strap position by stitching a rectangle.

6. Make double 1cm (½in) hems down the apron sides, tucking the waist ties in as you go. Sew in place. Finally turn and stitch a double 1cm (½in) hem at the apron bottom.

PROJECT VARIATION

Print the letters of your young chef's name in letters large enough to make sewing easy but small enough to fit on the apron. Use your printed letters as templates but remember to reverse them for the fusible appliqué! Appliqué the letters to the front of your apron and zigzag or straight stitch the letters in place before you construct the apron.

MEDIUM

KITCHEN SEAT CUSHIONS

Wooden kitchen chairs look great but are a total pain in the proverbial if you have to sit on them for any length of time. These smart tie-on cushions have a contrasting piped edge and ties, which add much-appreciated comfort, and even better, they don't need a zip!

YOU WILL NEED:

DRESSMAKER'S TISSUE

A PIECE OF HIGH DENSITY SEATING FOAM FOR EACH SEAT PAD, 1CM (½IN) THICK

FABRIC FOR THE TOP AND BOTTOM OF THE SEAT PAD (SEE ESTIMATING FABRIC BOX)

MATCHING SEWING THREAD

CONTRAST FABRIC FOR THE PIPING AND TIES

PIPING CORD LONG ENOUGH TO GO ROUND ALL THE EDGE OF THE SEAT PAD

1. Use your paper template (see Estimating Fabric box) to cut one seat pad from the foam. Now use your paper template to cut one seat top in your main fabric and set aside. Fold the remaining fabric in half, right sides together.

2. Fold the template in half, open out and measure 11cm (4½in) out from the fold; this overlap makes the envelope back. Fold at this point and use this new template to cut the back pieces from the folded fabric. Turn under a double 0.5cm (¼in) hem on each overlap and topstitch in place.

ESTIMATING FABRIC

Use a piece of dressmaker's tissue to make a paper template of your seat top. You can shape your cushion to fit around the back supports if you wish, it's not hard. Alternatively just make your pads to the shape of the main seat which is even easier. Add a 1cm (½in) seam allowance on all sides and cut out. You'll need one piece of fabric for the top of the seat pad and two pieces for the bottom, which will overlap by 10cm (4in) to make an envelope back.

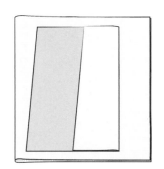

3. Cut strips of contrast fabric 5cm (2in) wide and sew end to end to make a strip long enough to cover the piping cord. Cover the piping cord (see Making and Applying Piping, page 37).

4. Make the ties. Each one is made from a strip of fabric 5x25cm (2x10in). Fold along the long edge, press and then fold the raw edges in to meet the centre fold; press again. Fold in one short end to neaten then topstitch around the edges. Make four ties for each cushion.

5. Assemble the cover. Lay the seat top fabric on your work surface, right side up. Lay two ties at each back corner, raw edges aligned. Position the covered piping around the entire perimeter, again raw edges aligned. Join the ends of the piping cord and the fabric covering the cord neatly (see page 37 if you need more guidance on this). Baste everything neatly in place.

6. Lay the two back sections on top, right sides facing down, so that they overlap by 10cm (4in) in the centre. Pin everything carefully together. Sew around the entire seat pad with a 1cm (½in) seam allowance.

7. Turn the seat pad cover through to the right side and insert the foam pad. Tie the seat pad to the kitchen chair.

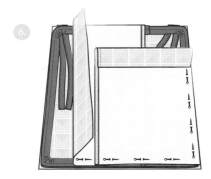

PROJECT VARIATION

If your kitchen chairs require drop-in seats, then make the Revamped Dining Room Chairs (see page 124).

MEDIUM

CAFÉ CURTAIN

I want my kitchen to be flooded with light but I also want privacy when I'm sitting at the kitchen table. The answer is a café curtain! Mine looks just as good from the outside as it does from inside the kitchen as the curtain is folded double. Clever eyelet heading tape, which you can buy from furnishing and curtain suppliers, make the curtains so very straightforward. Simply stitch the tape to the back of the curtain, cut away the fabric inside the rings and snap decorative eyelets onto the front. You'll be done in no time! A brass or chrome rod supports the curtain and fixes it to the inside of your window.

YOU WILL NEED:
CURTAIN FABRIC (SEE ESTIMATING FABRIC BOX)
MATCHING SEWING THREAD
EYELET CURTAIN TAPE TO FIT THE WIDTH OF YOUR CURTAIN – YOU GET
APPROXIMATELY 12 EYELET RINGS TO EVERY 1.5M (60IN) OF HEADING TAPE
SCISSORS
CHROME, BRASS OR COLOURED EYELET RINGS TO MATCH YOUR HEADING TAPE
CAFÉ CURTAIN ROD TO FIT YOUR WINDOW

1. Cut your fabric to the required width (see Estimating Fabric box), joining widths of fabric if necessary. Remember for the depth you need double the depth you want your curtain to be plus 2.5cm (1in).

ESTIMATING FABRIC

- *Measure the width of your window.*

- *Multiply this width by one and a half and add on 2.5cm (1in) for the side seams.*

- *Round this measurement up until you can fit an even number of eyelet rings across the width.*

- *For the depth you need to decide at what height you will hang the rod. For most windows, a depth of 38cm (15in) works well. You need twice this depth plus 2.5cm (1in) for seam allowances.*

2. Fold the fabric in half along the width, right sides together, and sew both side seams with 1cm (½in) seam allowances. Clip the corners. Sew across the long top edge towards the centre, leaving a gap that is 25cm (10in) unsewn for turning. Continue sewing to the end. Clip the top corners then turn the curtain through to the right side. Push out the corners and press.

3. Fold in the seam allowance on the centre 25cm (10in) and hand sew the gap closed. On the reverse side of the curtain, at the top edge, pin your eyelet heading tape across the top of the curtain, about 1cm (½in) from the curtain top. Make sure you tuck under the first and last 1cm (½in) of tape to neaten it. Stitch in place.

4. Carefully cut away the fabric in the centre of each ring completely. Use very sharp pointed scissors to give a neat edge.

5. Place the decorative eyelet ring over the hole, working from the front of the curtain. Ensure the fabric is smooth, press the ring down with firm pressure until the decorative ring on the front and the eyelet on the tape lock into place. Repeat this step for all the eyelet holes.

6. Fix the café rod brackets to the inside of the window surround, 38cm (15in) up from the windowsill. Slide the café curtain onto the rod, through the eyelets.

7. Fix the rod into place. Space the gathers evenly across your window.

PROJECT VARIATIONS

- *Make the curtain in two halves so that it can be drawn back neatly when you do not need that extra privacy.*

- *Sew trim along the bottom of your café curtain to add extra style.*

- *Add appliqués to the bottom edge of the café curtain for a fun and whimsical touch. Fold the curtain panel in half, right sides out and arrange your appliqués. Fuse in place then open the curtain panel out and sew around the appliqués. Refold the panel with the right sides together and continue as above.*

EVERYDAY PLACE MATS

These place mats might be 'everyday' but you can still make them fabulous with gorgeous fabric. The place mats are reversible with a pieced and a plain side. They are easy to wash and can be stored flat or rolled ready for the next mealtime.

YOU WILL NEED (FOR EACH PLACE MAT):
SIX SQUARES CREAM FABRIC, EACH 6X6CM (2½X2½IN)
SIX STRIPS DIFFERENT FABRICS, EACH 6X22CM (2½X8½IN)
MATCHING SEWING THREAD
PIECE PLAIN FABRIC, 39X34CM (15½X13½IN)
PIECE QUILT WADDING 39X34CM (15½X13½IN)

FINISHED SIZE: 30X25CM (12X10IN)

1. Sew the six cream fabric squares to one end of each of the strips then sew the strips together, alternating the position of the cream square to make a panel measuring 32x25cm (12½x10in).

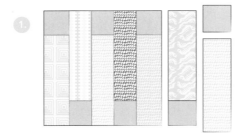

2. Layer the plain backing fabric, wrong side up, on your work surface then the wadding and then the pieced place mat on top, right side up, just as if you were making a quilt. The wadding and backing should be a few inches bigger all around.

3. Add some quilting lines along the pieced strips. I sewed wiggly lines through the centre of each strip. Experiment and don't worry if your lines of stitching aren't perfect. These lines of stitching hold your layers together and add decoration too. Make sure the threads are secured at the start and finish and snip them off neatly.

4. Trim the wadding carefully with scissors. You want it to be exactly the same size as the pieced top. Now carefully trim the plain backing so that it is 2.5cm (1in) bigger than the top and wadding all round. Turn the raw edge of this extra fabric in to meet the place mat top and press; then turn the folded edge over to 'bind' the raw edge. Pin in place. Do this on all four sides.

5. At the corners neatly fold a mitre on the right side (see Mitres, page 43).

6. Sew all around the 'binding' with a straight machine stitch to finish the edges of your place mat quickly and easily. This method can be used on quilts too!

PROJECT VARIATIONS

- *Make the front and back of the place mats from single pieces of fabric (not pieced) to make them even faster! Mark lines for quilting with an air-erasable marker pen.*

- *Appliqué fun shapes or names to the place mats to make them appealing to your younger (or not so young!) family members. Use fusible appliqué (see Fusible Appliqué, page 34) and let your imagination run riot!*

DRESSED-UP DINING
NICELY NEUTRAL

Let's be honest, most of us eat the majority of our meals in our kitchens, don't we? Meals in the dining room mean high days and holidays, Christmas, the boss coming round for dinner – formality. The following dining room projects are designed to bring some love back into this often-neglected room. Revamp those tired looking chairs or make a smart and practical tablecloth with a built-in table runner. For those times when you are entertaining, make the Fabric-embellished Place Cards (see page 126) to add a home-made touch to the setting. The look here is neutral to allow your culinary creations to shine but the designs would work with any colour palette. Be creative and have fun; it's time for the dining room to be a place to feast!

Re-vamped Dining Room Chairs 124

Fabric-embellished Place Cards 126

Simple Tablecloth 127

Napkins for All Seasons 130

Place Settings 132

Table Runner 135

**EASY
[NO SEW]**

REVAMPED DINING ROOM CHAIRS

If your dining room chairs are looking a little sad or don't play nicely with your gorgeous table setting then it's time to give them a makeover. Remove drop-in seats and lightly sand the chairs. Repaint with eggshell paint then get busy with the staple gun for a fabric lift that is little short of miraculous!

YOU WILL NEED:
SAD OR WEARY DINING CHAIRS WITH A DROP-IN SEAT
SANDPAPER AND EGGSHELL FINISH PAINT
75G (2OZ) POLYESTER QUILT WADDING (OPTIONAL)
STAPLE GUN AND STAPLES
SPRAY ADHESIVE
FABRIC FOR THE SEAT PAD (HOME DECORATING WEIGHT MAKES A STURDY COVER BUT DECENT CRAFT-WEIGHT FABRIC WILL DO A GREAT JOB TOO)

1. Remove the drop-in seat pad from your dining chair and set aside for the time being. Once your chair is sanded, dusted and repainted, let it dry.

2. If the pad needs a little extra padding cut a piece of quilt wadding that is a few cm/inches bigger than the seat pad all around. Wrap it over the pad, taking the wadding over the sides and stapling it neatly to the underside of the seat. Make sure the edges and corners are folded in really tight and flat so that the seat pad will still fit!

3. Spray the top and sides of the seat pad with adhesive, then stretch your cover fabric over it, making sure any motif or stripe runs straight. Neatly fold the corners, like making a bed and fold the excess fabric to the back of the seat pad.

4. Turn the seat pad upside down (underside facing up) and fold a neat double hem on one side. Pop a couple of staples in to hold it in place, then work on the opposite side, gently stretching the fabric to keep it taut. Fold the hem and staple. Repeat on the remaining two sides.

5. Once the cover is in place, tight enough and the fabric is straight you can add more staples, tightening the fabric where necessary to get a good finish. Once you're happy, push the seat pad back into place and get on with the others!

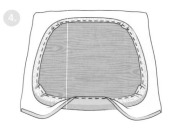

PROJECT VARIATION

If your dining chairs are solid wood then make the tie-on Kitchen Seat Cushions (see page 112).

**EASY
[NO SEW]**

FABRIC-EMBELLISHED PLACE CARDS

Use ready-made place cards, scraps of fabric and fusible web to create name cards for your dinner party or celebration. They take a few minutes to make and guests will enjoy taking their card home as a memento of a fabulous evening!

YOU WILL NEED:
SCRAPS OF PATTERNED FABRIC
READY-MADE PLACE CARDS
FUSIBLE WEB
SCISSORS
BUTTONS AND BEADS TO EMBELLISH (OPTIONAL)
HOT GLUE GUN (OPTIONAL)

1. Choose a motif from your fabric, making sure it is a suitable size to fit on your place card, and iron fusible web to the wrong side of the fabric.

2. Cut the motif out neatly with sharp scissors and remove the paper backing.

3. Fuse the motif to the place card, following the manufacturer's instructions.

4. Write your guest's name with pen or, if your motif is large and covers the card, use a permanent fabric-marking pen. Add buttons or beads to the motif using a hot glue gun if you wish.

PROJECT VARIATION

If your fabric does not have a suitable motif then trace a simple star, Christmas tree or flower shape onto the back of the fusible web, cut it out roughly, fuse it to the wrong side of your chosen fabric then cut it out neatly. Fuse to the card and embellish.

SIMPLE TABLECLOTH

When it comes to tablecloths I'm a big fan of plain and simple, but the brilliant thing about sewing your own is that you can have whatever you like. Go wild with extravagant florals or super-modern geometrics and if you need to join widths of fabric to achieve the size you need, then make those joined panels part of your design! You could even use strips and scraps from other projects to make a patchwork tablecloth, just neaten all raw edges with a zigzag stitch so that seams will stand up to regular laundering!

YOU WILL NEED:
FABRIC FOR THE TABLECLOTH (SEE ESTIMATING FABRIC BOX)
MATCHING SEWING THREAD
CURTAIN WEIGHTS (OPTIONAL)

1. Cut a panel of fabric to your required size, joining widths if necessary. For example, if your table top was 135x185cm (54x74in) you would need a finished tablecloth of 175x225cm (70x90in). This includes the 20cm (8in) overhang on all sides. You also need to add on 5cm (2in) to both sides for hems so the panel would need to be cut 180x230cm (72x92in). You could cut two panels of the same fabric, each 91x230cm (36½x92in) and join them but you will have to match the patterns carefully.

2. I prefer this method: cut three panels, one patterned and two plain and make a striped cloth with a 'runner' effect down the centre. The centre runner is cut from a bold patterned fabric, 62.5x230cm (25x92in), and the two side panels are cut from plain fabric, 61x230cm (24½x92in). Join the three strips, overlock or zigzag stitch the seams then press them towards the centre fabric. Much easier and, I think, this creates more of an impact! What's not to love about that?

ESTIMATING FABRIC

- *Measure the length and width of your tabletop and add 40cm (16in) to both measurements. A tablecloth should have a minimum drape of 20cm (8in) on all sides to hang nicely but for real extravagant luxury why not take your tablecloth to the floor!*

- *You'll also need to add 5cm (2in) to both sides for hems.*

- *If you're joining widths of fabric include 1cm (½in) seam allowances for them too.*

3. Turn a 1cm (½in) seam on all sides and press, then turn a second 1cm (½in) hem in on one side. Fold the corner in to meet this hem then turn under the adjacent hem to make a mitre; pin carefully (see Mitres, page 43). Repeat on all four corners.

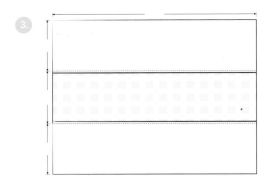

4. Machine stitch the hem in place using a straight stitch.

5. If you want the corners to be weighted, simply fold and stitch a hemmed triangle of fabric to the corners and slip a curtain weight inside. Slip stitch the top of this little pocket closed by hand to keep the weight securely inside!

Stuart's Tip

For a super easy tablecloth that would also work well in the kitchen, just cut a piece of oilcloth to the size required (see Estimating Fabric box, page 127). The edges of oilcloth can be left unsewn but if you want to smarten them up use a matching sewing thread and either a walking or teflon foot on your sewing machine to hem the edges.

PROJECT VARIATION

If you want to make a circular tablecloth you will need to make a paper pattern first. Measure the diameter of your table and halve it. Now add on 20cm (8in) for the overhang and 2.5cm (1in) for seam allowances. Make a pencil and string 'compass' to this length and draw a circle on dressmaker's tissue paper. Cut out this paper template and use it to cut your fabric. Make double folded seams, stitch and you're done!

NAPKINS FOR ALL SEASONS

Napkins are a really easy way to bring style to the dining table and with a simple change of fabric, can look radically different. I love to use fabrics from a coordinating range and then mix them up for a mismatched look, which still blends beautifully. These napkins are made extra fancy by being double-sided – even more chances to use beautiful fabrics!

YOU WILL NEED:
50X50CM (20X20IN) MAIN/OUTER FABRIC
45X45CM (18X18IN) INNER/LINING FABRIC
QUILT BASTING SPRAY, SUCH AS 505 (OPTIONAL)
MATCHING SEWING THREAD
FINISHED SIZE: EACH NAPKIN IS 45X45CM (18X18IN)

1. Place the larger (main fabric) square on your work surface, wrong side facing up and place your smaller square (lining fabric) on top of it, right in the centre, wrong sides together. There should be a 2.5cm (1in) border of the main fabric on all sides.

2. Pin the centre square or use quilt basting spray to hold it in place. Turn a 1cm (½in) hem in on all sides, bringing the raw edges of the larger square in to meet the raw edges of the smaller square and press. Next turn two opposing side hems in another 1cm (½in), covering the raw edge of the smaller square by 1cm (½in), and press.

3. Fold one of the corners in until it is level with the double folded hem, then fold the single hem in 1cm (½in) to form a neat mitre at the corner. Pin, then repeat on all four corners.

4. Pin your hems in place and check that the napkin is a precise 45cm (18in) square.

5. Topstitch very close to the double folded hem in one continuous line, backstitching at the beginning and end to secure your threads. Use a straight stitch or, for more interest, use one (or more) of your sewing machine's decorative stitches.

Stuart's Tip

For really easy, casual napkins, see how to make the Everyday Napkins, page 99.

PROJECT VARIATIONS

- *Use a black-and-white print on the outside and a pop of vibrant colour (lime green, fuchsia, canary yellow) for a modern, striking look on the inside.*

- *For festive napkins, pair two Christmas fabrics together: a large-scale print on the outside and a smaller-scale print for the lining. Topstitch with gold metallic thread!*

- *Use fusible appliqué or the embroidery function on your sewing machine to personalise the napkins and they become place cards too! Add your guests' names to the outer napkin before you sew the two parts together for a neat, professional finish that looks good on both sides. Give your guests their napkins at the end of the meal.*

MEDIUM

PLACE SETTINGS

These large place settings are multi-functional: there's a space for cutlery to create lots of impact on a plain table or simple tablecloth. Alter the size to fit your available space but make sure that your largest dinner plate will fit comfortably.

YOU WILL NEED:

45CM (18IN) MAIN FABRIC

45CM (18IN) COORDINATING FABRIC FOR THE BACKING

90CM (36IN) SECOND COORDINATING FABRIC FOR THE BINDING, CUTLERY HOLDER

45CM (18IN) MEDIUM-WEIGHT IRON-ON INTERFACING

MATCHING SEWING THREAD

FINISHED SIZE: MAKES THREE SETTINGS, EACH 45X30CM (18X12IN)

1. Cut one panel from the main fabric and one from the co-ordinating backing, both 46x31cm (18½x12½in). Cut two strips from the second coordinating fabric, each 6cm (2½in) by the width of the fabric for the binding. Cut a panel that is 14x32.5cm (5½x13in) for the cutlery holder, also from the second coordinating fabric. Cut the interfacing to the same size as the cutlery holder and fuse it to the wrong side of the fabric for the cutlery holder.

2. Mark straight lines on the right side of your main fabric panel. Layer the panel with a piece of wadding and the backing fabric, right sides out to make a quilt sandwich. Quilt along the marked lines (see Machine Quilting, page 48).

3. Sew the binding strips together and use to bind the place setting (see Machine Sewn Binding, page 48).

4. Make the cutlery pocket. Fold the interfaced piece of fabric in half, right sides together, to make a folded piece that is 14x16cm (5½x6½in). Sew the side seams using 1cm (½in) seam allowances, clip the corners, then turn through to the right side and press. The folded edge is the top of your pocket. Topstitch a line 0.5cm (¼in) away from the folded edge. Turn the bottom edge under by 1cm (½in) to make a neat bottom hem then pin the pocket onto the left-hand side of the place setting. The left-hand edge of the pocket should be 2.5cm (1in) in from the binding and the bottom of the pocket should be 2.5cm (1in) up from the bottom edge. Pin the pocket in place then topstitch around three sides to attach it to the place mat. The finished pocket should be 11cm (4½in) wide.

5. Make a napkin to coordinate. Place cutlery in the pocket and you're ready to entertain!

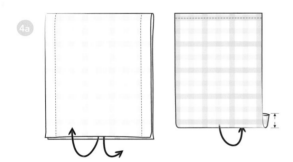

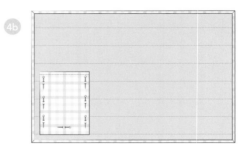

TABLE RUNNER

Table runners are ace; they add a pop of colour and pattern to an otherwise plain table or add even more pattern and texture to your scheme. Running down the centre of the table they are really useful for dishes and serving platters. Running across the table they can take the place of two place mats or table settings. This runner is very straightforward and can easily be made to match your dining, kitchen or garden accessories. There are options for taking it further if you want something more challenging too! Use 0.5cm (¼in) seam allowances throughout.

YOU WILL NEED:

APPROXIMATELY 45CM (18IN) FABRIC IN TOTAL TO PIECE THE RUNNER CENTRE. I USED A VARIETY OF SCRAPS AND STRIPS, AT LEAST 76CM (30½IN) LONG, AND IN WIDTHS BETWEEN 4CM (1½IN) AND 8CM (3IN) WIDE

45CM (18IN) FABRIC FOR THE ACCENT BANDS AND THE BINDING

45CM (18IN) FABRIC FOR THE RUNNER ENDS

RIC RAC BRAID (OPTIONAL)

160X48CM (64X19IN) WADDING (I USED THERMAL INSULATING WADDING)

160X48CM (64X19IN) BACKING FABRIC

MATCHING THREADS FOR SEWING AND QUILTING

FINISHED SIZE: 150X38CM (60X15IN)

1. Cut your fabric scraps for the pieced centre into lengths that are 76cm (30½in) long and between 4cm (1½in) and 8cm (3in) wide. Sew the strips together to create a pieced panel that is 76x39cm (30½x15½in), trimming to size if necessary.

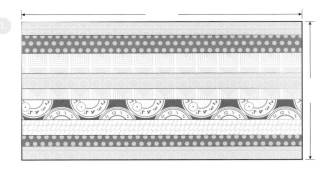

2. Cut two strips from your accent/binding fabric that are each 6x39cm (2½x15½in) and sew one to each end of the pieced panel. Press the seam allowances towards the accent strip.

3. Cut two panels from the runner end fabric, each 39x34cm (15½x13½in) and sew one to either end of the runner. Press the seam allowances towards the runner ends. Sew the ric rac braid along the middle of the accent strips, if using.

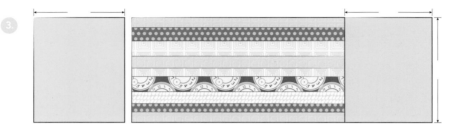

4. Layer the top of the runner with the wadding and backing fabric and quilt as desired (see Layering a Quilt Sandwich, page 46). I quilted along the piecing lines; I also quilted vertical lines in the runner ends.

5. Trim the backing fabric and wadding even with the runner top. Cut three 6cm (2½in) strips of binding fabric and sew them end to end. Use this strip to bind the runner (see Binding a Quilt, page 49).

PROJECT VARIATIONS

- *Use a wide striped fabric for the runner ends.*

- *Add appliqué to the runner ends for a more challenging project. Follow the instructions for using fusible web (see page 34), then machine blanket stitch, satin stitch or zigzag the appliqué edges for durability.*

BEDROOM BLISS
ROMANTIC OR SHABBY CHIC

For my money, a bedroom should be a haven of tranquillity and peace, a refuge from the stresses of the real world and a place to escape to when life gets a bit too intense. Bedrooms are the perfect room to indulge your need for plump cushions and piles of pillows, a comforting quilt to wrap yourself in and beautiful accessories to complete your haven. To achieve this look, I have combined a glorious feature fabric, printed with huge cabbage roses with smaller floral sprig prints, polka dots and a ticking stripe with plenty of white, pastel pink and baby blue for a look that is soft and romantic without being dated. There's a gorgeous big bed quilt, piles of matching pillow shams and cushions, fun accessories and even a revamped faux headboard if, like mine, yours is more shabby than chic! If faded florals aren't your thing, any of the fabric schemes from this book would work in the bedroom. Modern brights, funky retro, country cosy, New England coastal, masculine, juvenile – in a bedroom anything (and I mean anything) goes. Steady!

Faux Headboard 142

Basic Pillowcases 144

Pretty Patchwork Cushions 146

Embellished Pillowcases 149

Drawstring Laundry or Pyjama Bag 152

Patchwork Eye Mask 156

Box-pleated Bed Valance 159

Quilted Cushion 162

Patchwork Quilt 165

FAUX HEADBOARD

*Give a bed a more tailored look with this faux headboard made from large artists'
canvases. There's absolutely no sewing involved and the whole thing will take you
less than an hour.*

YOU WILL NEED:
LARGE ARTISTS' CANVASES MOUNTED ONTO FRAMES (I USED TWO, EACH
60X75CM (24X30IN)
FABRIC PANELS LARGE ENOUGH TO COVER THE FRAMES WITH 5CM (2IN) EXTRA
ON ALL SIDES
STAPLE GUN
HANGING WALL HOOKS
**FINISHED SIZE: EACH PANEL IS 60X75CM (24X30IN). TWO OF THESE MAKE
A GREAT HEADBOARD FOR A DOUBLE BED BUT YOU CAN BUY READY-MADE
ARTISTS' CANVASES IN A VARIETY OF SIZES.**

1. Cut the fabric to size. Do this by measuring the artists' canvas frames
   and adding 5cm (2in) extra on all sides to allow for folding over.

2. Stretch the fabric over the frames and staple neatly in place on the
   back. Work from top to bottom first, smoothing out the fabric neatly
   as you go.

3. When the top and bottom ends are stapled repeat with the sides,
   folding the corners into neat mitres and stapling to secure. Repeat for
   all your headboard panels.

4. Fix hooks to the wall behind the bed and hang your faux headboard
   panels side by side for amazing impact in less than an hour.

BASIC PILLOWCASES

The first of two patterns for pillowcases, this is the most basic and uses just one piece of fabric. It's well worth using a really good-quality cotton here so the pillowcases will launder well and stay looking good! Just like a bought pillowcase, this one has a built-in flap to tuck your pillow into and durable, overlocked seams. Unlike its factory-made equivalent, your pillowcases can be made in any fabric to match or contrast with your bedroom décor. Pillowcases are fun and quick to make and have that 'aha!' moment when you turn them right sides out.

YOU WILL NEED:
180CM (72IN) OF 100–110CM (40–42IN) WIDE COTTON OR LINEN BLENDED FABRIC
MATCHING SEWING THREAD

FINISHED SIZE: MAKES TWO STANDARD PILLOWCASES, EACH 48X72.5CM (19X29IN)

1. For each pillowcase cut a panel of fabric that measures 50x168cm (20x67in). As you are working with the lengthwise grain of the fabric, it makes sense to make your pillowcases in pairs; in which case, cut two panels.

2. On one short end fold and press a 2.5cm (1in) hem then turn over a further 5cm (2in) hem and press. Pin the hem and topstitch close to the fold with matching sewing thread.

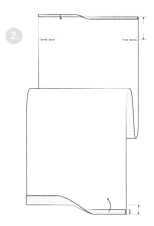

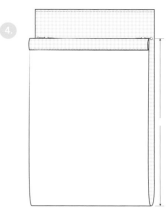

3. On the other short end of the same panel turn under a 1cm (½in) hem and press. Turn the hem under another 1cm (½in), press and pin. Topstitch close to the fold. Place a pin 12.5cm (5in) down from this upper edge on both long sides. The top 12.5cm (5in) will form the tuck-in end.

4. With right sides facing you and the tuck-in end at the top, fold the bottom (with the 5cm/2in hem) up towards the upper edge until it meets the pins. Measure your folded part; it should be 72.5cm (29in) to the pins with the 12.5cm (5in) tuck-in at the top.

5. Now fold the 12.5cm (5in) tuck-in (with the 1cm/½in hem) down over the pillowcase. Pin the side seams.

6. Sew the side seams using a 1cm (½in) seam allowance. Trim off the corners close to the stitching to reduce bulk. Overlock or zigzag stitch the side seams to make them durable and to reduce fraying.

7. Turn the pillowcase through to the right side through the top opening. Push out the corners with a point turner or chopstick and press well. Insert your standard pillow and plump!

Stuart's Tip

You can also make pillowcases that are unusual sizes, such as a king size 48x90cm (19x36in).

**EASY/
MEDIUM**

PRETTY PATCHWORK CUSHIONS

Lots of pretty strips are sewn together to create this beautiful bedroom cushion. Cotton bobble trim adds a smart designer touch, while an easy envelope back makes this a straightforward project you can whip up in next to no time.

YOU WILL NEED:

STRIPS OF FABRIC AT LEAST 30CM (12IN) LONG AND IN VARIOUS WIDTHS, FROM 4–8CM (1½–3IN)

TWO PANELS OF FABRIC FOR THE ENVELOPE BACK, EACH 30X32.5CM (12X13IN)

MATCHING SEWING THREAD

APPROXIMATELY 60CM (24IN) COTTON BOBBLE TRIM

28X50CM (11X20IN) CUSHION PAD

FINISHED SIZE: 28X50CM (11X20IN)

1. Sew your strips of fabric together down the long 30cm (12in) sides using 0.5cm (¼in) seam allowances and varying the width of the strips until you have a piece of 'patchwork' fabric that is approximately 30x52.5cm (12x21in). Trim your patchwork fabric to this size if necessary.

2. Make the envelope back. Take one panel of backing fabric and turn under a 1cm (½in) hem along one 30cm (12in) side. Press and turn under again to make a double hem. Topstitch along this hem with matching sewing thread. Repeat with the other backing piece.

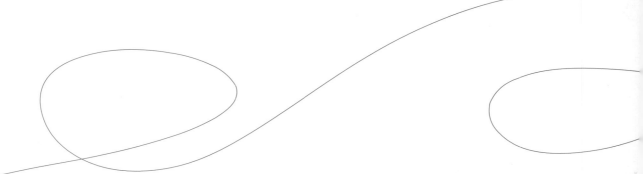

3. Cut your bobble trim into two lengths, each 30cm (12in) long.

4. Place your patchwork panel right sides up in front of you. Lay the bobble trim along each short end with the bobbles facing inwards. Lay a backing piece on top, right sides down. The hemmed edge should be somewhere near the middle of your patchwork top and the raw end should be even with the bobble trim end. Lay the other backing piece on top, right sides down again at the other end. The two hemmed edges should overlap in the centre. Pin all around the outer edges making sure that the edges and the bobble trim are all neatly pinned together.

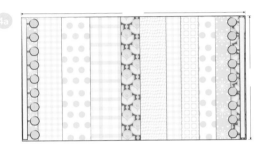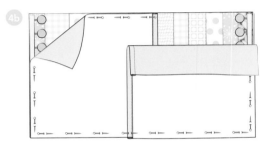

5. Sew all around the outer edges of your cushion cover, this time using a 1cm (½in) seam allowance. Turn your cushion cover through to the right side and make sure that everything is as it should be. Check that the envelope back is in place securely and the bobble trim is neatly applied. If it isn't, unpick and have another go. You really don't want to try unpicking an overlocked edge so for the sake of checking, it really is worth it! If everything looks lovely, turn it back inside out, trim off the corners and overlock or zigzag the raw outer edges.

6. Turn the cushion cover back through to the right side, push the corners out with a point turner or a chopstick and press. Insert your cushion pad.

PROJECT VARIATIONS

- *You can adapt this method to any size or shape of cushion; just sew fabric strips together and trim them down to the size required for the front.*

- *I like approximately 8–10cm (3–4in) of overlap on an envelope back. Any less and your cushion back may bulge open, revealing the cushion pad.*

- *If you don't want a patchwork front just cut a panel that is 30x52.5cm (12x21in) from a single fabric.*

- *Replace the bobble trim with a beaded trim, tassel trim or leave the trim out altogether!*

EMBELLISHED PILLOWCASES

The great thing about making your own pillowcases is that you can make them in any colour combination you like. I used fabrics from the Patchwork Quilt (see page 165) to make these pillowcases: the main fabric is the large rose print, the folded band is in contrasting bright gingham and the end and tuck-in is a taupe polka dot print. They don't take much longer to make than the standard plain pillowcase but add a real designer touch!

YOU WILL NEED:
50X134CM (20X53½IN) PANEL OF MAIN FABRIC (A)
50X10CM (20X4IN) CONTRAST FABRIC FOR THE FOLDED INSERT (B)
50X35CM (20X14IN) CONTRAST FABRIC FOR THE PILLOW END AND TUCK-IN (C)
MATCHING SEWING THREAD

FINISHED SIZE: MAKES TWO STANDARD PILLOWCASES, EACH 48X72.5CM (19X29IN)

1. Cut your fabrics to the above dimensions. Remember the long main panel is cut on the length of the fabric so it makes sense to make a pair of pillowcases to make best use of the fabric. At one short end of the main fabric make a hem by folding and pressing 2.5cm (1in) then 5cm (2in) as for the Basic Pillowcases (see page 144). Pin and then topstitch close to the fold.

2. Take the smaller piece of contrast fabric (B) and fold it in half down the long edge so it is 50x5cm (20x2in); press. Lay the folded strip at the top of the main fabric (A), right sides together and with raw edges lined up. Baste the folded strip in place.

3. Take the other piece of contrast fabric (C) and fold in a 1cm (½in) hem on one longer side; press and repeat and then topstitch – this is the tuck-in edge. Measure 12.5cm (5in) down from this hemmed edge and place a pin at either side to mark the top tuck-in.

4. Lay this contrast panel (C) on top of the main panel, right sides together and matching the remaining raw 50cm (20in) edge with the basted raw edge of the main panel; pin. Sew main panel A to contrast panel C with the folded piece B sandwiched in between, using a 1cm (½in) seam allowance. Overlock or zigzag this seam.

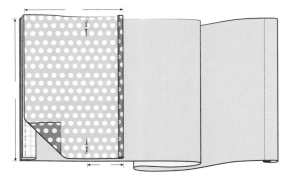

5.   Turn your fabric right sides up and press the folded contrast band (B) towards fabric C. You might like to baste the folded band in place for extra security.

6.   Place the pillowcase panel in front of you with right sides facing you and the tuck-in end at the top. Fold the bottom hem up towards the upper edge until it meets the pins. Measure your folded part, it should be 72.5cm (29in) to the pins with the 12.5cm (5in) tuck-in at the top.

7.   Now fold the tuck in down over the pillowcase and pin the side seams. Sew the side seams using a 1cm (½in) seam allowance. Trim off the corners close to the stitching line to eliminate bulk and then overlock or zigzag the side seams.

8.   Turn the pillowcase right sides out, push out the corners with a point turner or chopstick and press. Insert your pillow and plump!

PROJECT VARIATIONS

- *Vary the width of the inserted strip. Just decide how wide you want the folded strip, double this measurement and add 2.5cm (1in) to the final measurement for seam allowances.*

- *The folded strip could easily be replaced with a piece of lace edging or a fine flanged cord or homemade piping, inserted between fabrics A and C. In this case the trim will not need to be folded.*

- *Upcycle vintage linen tablecloths and sheets, often to be found at bargain prices in antique and bric-à-brac shops. Vintage linens often have lace or embroidered panels, which could be given a whole new lease of life!*

- *Add embroidery or appliqué to your pillowcases or embellish ready-made ones. If you're adding appliqué make sure the edges are securely finished so that your linens will withstand regular laundering.*

- *If you add embellishments make sure they are soft and comfortable to sleep on. No one wants to wake up with the imprint of a button on their face!*

DRAWSTRING LAUNDRY OR PYJAMA BAG

Even untidy teens can be encouraged to pick their dirty clothes off the floor when they have a lovely laundry bag in which to put the offending items. You may need to show your teen how to do this a couple of times but trust me they will learn! This bag will also house a pair of pyjamas beautifully. It also works as a sports kit bag, toy bag, Christmas present sack or why not store rolled quilts in it over the summer? Scaled down this handy bag becomes an ace gadget bag, shaving sack, shoe bag or even a little bag for your sunglasses.

YOU WILL NEED:
APPROXIMATELY TWELVE FABRIC SCRAPS THAT ARE 16CM (6½IN) WIDE AND BETWEEN 16CM (6½IN) AND 21CM (8½IN) LONG
137CM (54IN) PLAIN WHITE FABRIC
WHITE SEWING THREAD
3.2M (3½YD) OF 2CM (¾IN) WIDE SATIN RIBBON
YOU'LL ALSO NEED ROTARY CUTTING EQUIPMENT (SEE PAGE 27)

FINISHED SIZE: 48X25CM (19X10IN)

1. Join the short (16cm/6½in) ends of your fabric scraps to each other until you have a strip that's at least 60cm (24in) long. Make four of these strips in total. Press the seam allowances neatly to one side.

2. If you like, add some decorative stitching along the right side of the seam lines. It's an opportunity to have a play with your sewing machine and see what it can do. The decorative stitches will look pretty and they will make the seams more durable. Two for one!

3. Join the strips of patchwork together along the 60cm (24in) sides. Again, press your seam allowances neatly to one side and add some decorative stitches if you like.

4. Press your patchwork piece, then use your rotary cutting equipment to trim the panel to a rectangle that is 60x55cm (24x22in).

5. From your white fabric cut a total of three panels, each 60x55cm (24x22in). One of them is for the back of the bag and the other two are the lining pieces. If you want, the back of the bag could also be patchwork or a single piece of pretty fabric, it's up to you!

6. Take your patchwork panel and the back piece of your bag and place them right sides together with the shorter (55cm/22in) edge at the top. Use a ruler or tape measure to measure 8cm (3in) down from the top and place a mark at either side. Pin from the first mark down one side, across the bottom and up the other side to the other mark. Do exactly the same with the two lining pieces.

7. Sew around the pinned edges of the bag outer and bag lining, from mark to mark. Clip off the bottom corners and press the seam allowances open. Also press the unsewn 8cm (3in) part of each bag open and stitch around this 'V' shape as shown.

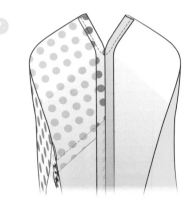

8. Turn the bag outer right sides out and press both the outer and the lining. Place the lining inside the bag outer so that the wrong sides are together and the top raw edges match. Pin and sew along both raw edges.

9. Turn the top down just past the stitching line, press, then turn the folded edge down to meet the bottom of the 'V' to make the drawstring casing. Pin in place.

10. Sew around the bottom edge of the casing close to the folded edge. Do the same around the top of the casing. Remember to keep your bag open all the time otherwise you'll sew up the opening – it's easily done, trust me!

11. Cut your length of ribbon in half and attach a safety pin to the end of one piece; this will help you thread it through the casing. Starting at one side, go all the way round until you get back to the start. Even out the ribbon and knot the ends together. Now take the other piece of ribbon and, starting at the other side of the bag casing, thread it through using the safety pin. Knot the ends.

12. Pull the ribbons to close the bag and . . . hey presto! Now pick those dirty socks up off the floor, put them in the bag and get that bedroom tidy!

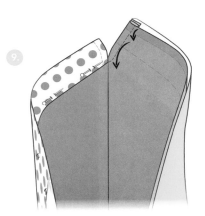

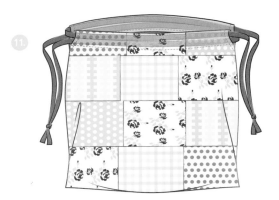

MEDIUM

PATCHWORK EYE MASK

I love an eye mask! Whenever I fly I pop one in my hand luggage and use it instead of the awful, thin nylon version the airlines always dole out. It's comfy and of course it blocks out light, ensuring a restful sleep. It's a boon for daytime naps too or for use when you're staying in a hotel room with unlined curtains.

YOU WILL NEED:
NINE SMALL SCRAPS OF ASSORTED PRETTY FLORAL FABRICS, EACH 4CM (1½IN) WIDE AND APPROXIMATELY 12.5CM (5IN) LONG
MATCHING SEWING THREAD
25X12.5CM (10X5IN) BACKING FABRIC
8X38CM (3X15IN) FABRIC FOR THE HEAD STRAP
35CM (14IN) ELASTIC, 1CM (½IN) WIDE
25X12.5CM (10X5IN) QUILT WADDING
EYE MASK PATTERN PIECE A (SEE PAGE 59), CUT OUT IN TISSUE PAPER
FINISHED SIZE: APPROXIMATELY 18X8CM (7X3IN)

1. Using a 0.5cm (¼in) seam allowance throughout, sew your nine floral scraps together along the 12.5cm (5in) sides to make a piece of fabric that is 12.5cm (5in) wide and 24cm (9½in) long. Press all your seam allowances neatly to the same side and clip off any untidy threads.

2. Take your piece of backing fabric and cut it in half to yield two 12.5cm (5in) squares. Sew the two squares back together, backstitching at the beginning and end leaving a gap in the middle about 5cm (2in) long. Press the seam allowances open, including the unjoined section in the middle.

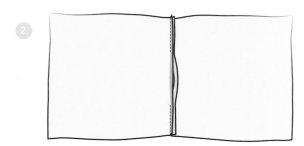

3. Measure round your head from temple to temple and add 2.5cm (1in) for seam allowances. Mine is 45cm (18in), plus the seam allowance, but I do have a big head; yours may be smaller so adjust accordingly. Cut your fabric for the head strap to this length by 8cm (3in) wide. Fold the strip in half lengthwise and press, then fold the long raw edges in towards the middle and press again. You should have a strip that's 2cm (¾in) wide.

4. Tuck your elastic inside this strip. Don't panic if it isn't the same length: get one end to match up and sew a few times across the end to secure the elastic inside the head strap. Now do the same at the other end. Next topstitch along the long edge of your strap with a matching colour and as you sew keep a hold of the end of your strap and stretch the elastic to fit. Secure your line of topstitching by backstitching at the end.

5. Lay your patchwork fabric right sides up in front of you, next lay the elasticated strap on top with the raw edges matched up to the short raw edges of the patchwork – a pin will help keep them in place. Next lay down the wadding then the backing fabric with the join in the middle, right sides down. Finally pin pattern piece A on top with the centre line on the pattern matched up with the opening on your backing.

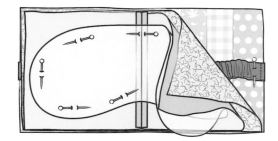

6. Sew all around pattern piece A with your sewing machine. Remove the pattern piece and trim around your stitching line with a 0.5cm (¼in) seam allowance. Turn the eye mask through to the right side and slip stitch the opening in the backing fabric neatly by hand.

PROJECT VARIATIONS

- *You could make the front of the eye mask in one single fabric if you prefer, just cut a piece the same size as your backing.*

- *If you don't want to cover your elasticated head strap you don't have to!*

- *If you like to embroider, why not make the eye mask front in a plain fabric and embroider two eyes: closed . . . open . . . one of each?*

- *My version is sweet and girly but you can butch this one up with a plain navy or black cotton fabric . . . even tough guys need to sleep!*

BOX-PLEATED BED VALANCE

A bed valance or dust ruffle hides a multitude of sins, from an ugly divan base to utilitarian under-bed storage boxes. Books, magazines and other bits and bobs can be tucked away under the ruffle out of sight but don't be surprised if your teenager 'tidies' their room by simply shoving everything under the bed. It also does, as the name suggests, a great job of preventing dust accumulating under the bed. Use 1cm (½in) seam allowances throughout.

YOU WILL NEED:

PLAIN SHEETING OR RECYCLED PLAIN SHEET (YOU COULD 'CHEAT' AND USE A READY-MADE/INEXPENSIVE/EXISTING BED VALANCE AND REMOVE THE RUFFLE)
FABRIC FOR YOUR RUFFLE (SEE ESTIMATING FABRIC BOX)
MATCHING SEWING THREAD

1. Cut the plain or recycled sheeting for the top piece to size (see Estimating Fabric box). Mark the centre of both long sides with a notch snipped into the seam allowance.

2. Cut your fabric for the ruffle (see Estimating Fabric box). You will need to join pieces to achieve the required length so overlock or zigzag stitch the seams to prevent fraying.

ESTIMATING FABRIC

- *To find the size of the top piece measure the width and the length of the bed base (without the mattress) and add 1cm (½in) to all sides for seam allowances.*

- *To find the depth of the ruffle measure from the top of the bed base to the floor and add on 1cm (½in) for the seam and 2.5cm (1in) for the bottom hem.*

- *To find the length of the ruffle, measure along one long side of the bed, double it and then add on the length of one short side of the bed. You will need to add 20cm (8in) for the top of the bed (10cm/4in on either side). To this length you will need to add extra for the box pleats. I allow 15cm (6in) for each box pleat; on a double bed I put one at each corner and one on either long side, making six pleats that require an additional 90cm (36in) extra fabric. For a king size bed you could have two box pleats per long side and one on the short side if you wish. The extra 'give' that the pleats add allows for easy access under the bed.*

3. On the lower edge of the ruffle turn under a 1cm (½in) hem, press and repeat to make a double hem. Topstitch the hem with matching sewing thread and neaten the short side edges with an overlock or zigzag stitch.

4. With right sides together and the raw edges aligned, start sewing the ruffle to the top piece. Start 10cm (4in) from the top corner. Make a box pleat at the corner as shown. To make a box pleat using 15cm (6in) of fabric, place pins at the start and end of the 15cm (6in). Now find the centre point (8cm/3in) and place a pin. Place a pin 2.5cm/1in on either side of this centre mark (at 5cm/2in and 10cm/4in). These last two pin marks should be brought into the centre mark and pinned in place, forming a letter 'S' at either side. This forms the box pleat. Each box pleat uses 15cm (6in) of fabric.

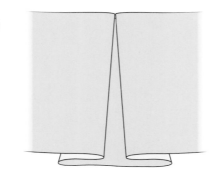

5. Continue sewing to the first notch (halfway down the long side) and then make another box pleat. Continue working round the top piece, making box pleats at each corner and in the centre of the other long side. Overlock or zigzag stitch the raw edges to neaten them.

PROJECT VARIATIONS

- *Use a fabric that complements or matches your bedding. A vertical stripe always looks smart but make sure you match the patterns carefully when you join pieces.*

- *For a gathered dust ruffle cut the skirt fabric to twice the total length (two long edges plus one short edge plus 20cm (8in) for the top edge) then gather with a long running stitch by hand. Gather the ruffles to the required length then sew on with a 1cm (½in) seam allowance as before.*

- *Add trim or ribbon to the lower edge for a dash of colour!*

QUILTED CUSHION

A pile of plump coordinating cushions atop one's bed makes a comforting nest to retreat to when the world gets too much. This quilted cushion is a generous 50cm (20in) square, and is made using a spare block from the Patchwork Quilt (see page 165). If you're considering making the quilt, make the cushion first as it is super quick and a great way to practice the block and quilt techniques needed. Width of Fabric, or WOF, is in most cases between 105cm (42in) for cotton quilting fabrics and 137cm (54in) for home furnishing fabrics.

YOU WILL NEED:
32.5CM (13IN) X WOF MEDIUM-SCALE ROSE PRINT FABRIC
8CM (3IN) X WOF TINY PINK POLKA DOT PRINT FABRIC
MATCHING SEWING AND QUILTING THREADS
16CM (6½IN) SQUARE LARGE-SCALE FLORAL PRINT FABRIC
90CM (36IN) PLAIN WHITE FABRIC FOR THE QUILT BACKING AND THE CUSHION BACK
QUILT BASTING SPRAY, SUCH AS 505
55CM (22IN) SQUARE QUILT WADDING
50CM (20IN) SQUARE CUSHION PAD
YOU'LL ALSO NEED ROTARY CUTTING EQUIPMENT (SEE PAGE 27)

FINISHED SIZE: 50X50CM (20X20IN)

1. From the medium-scale rose print fabric cut four pieces, each 16x34cm (6½x13½in). From the tiny polka dot print fabric cut four strips, each 4x34cm (1½x13½in). Sew one of these strips onto one long side of a medium-scale rose print strip. Press the seam allowance towards the wider strip. Make four in total.

2. Using the block construction technique from the Patchwork Quilt (see page 165), make one block using the partial seam allowance method. Press all seam allowances towards the centre square.

3. From the plain white fabric cut one 55cm (22in) square and two rectangles each 51.5x34cm (20½x13½in). Lay the white fabric square on the table, wrong side up and spray with quilt basting spray. Lay the wadding on top and smooth out any wrinkles, spray the wadding with basting spray and finally put the patchwork block on top, right side facing up. Centre the patchwork block; there should be about 2.5cm (1in) of wadding and backing extra round each of the sides. Make sure the patchwork top is nice and flat, smooth and firmly attached.

4. Quilt the patchwork block (see Machine Quilting, page 48). When you have finished quilting, trim the wadding and backing so it is even with the quilt top.

5. To make the envelope back, take one of the 51.5x34cm (20½x13½in) rectangles of white fabric and fold a 1cm (½in) hem on one short side, press and then fold over again to make a double hem. Topstitch the hem with matching thread. Do exactly the same with the other rectangle of white fabric.

6. Lay one hemmed rectangle on top of the quilted cushion front, right sides together and hemmed edge in the centre. Lay the second hemmed rectangle on top, again right sides down so that the two hemmed edges overlap in the centre. Pin all around the outer edges of the cushion cover.

7. Using a 0.5cm (¼in) seam allowance, sew all around the outer edges. Trim off the corners and overlock or zigzag the raw edges. Turn the quilted cushion cover right sides out and insert your square cushion pad.

PROJECT VARIATIONS

- *I like to use feather cushion pads because they have a lovely plump squashiness to them but polyester fibrefill is another option. Both are machine washable and durable and both are readily available. Fibrefill is a better option if any of your family have allergies.*

- *Any of the cushions in the book could be layered with wadding and backing and quilted before they are made up into cushions. Adding wadding gives the fabric more substance and the quilting adds a wonderful texture. It's also a great opportunity to practice your machine quilting on something small and manageable. Layering and quilting will also enclose all the raw edges on a pieced or patchwork cushion front and make the whole cushion more durable and better able to withstand laundering.*

- *Add bobble trim to the edges, tassels to the corners or piping round the outside if you wish.*

- *Add covered buttons and buttonholes to the envelope back for an even smarter finish. It's also a great opportunity to practice machine buttonholes if you want to!*

PATCHWORK QUILT

Patchwork quilts are really what started my love affair with sewing. There is something incredibly satisfying about making one, owning one, sleeping under one. I designed this quilt pattern to work at any size and with any fabric range. The blocks are big, 50cm (20in) square, so this quilt will grow fast . . . I made the whole quilt top in eight hours! If you've never made a quilt before, this project will challenge you, but don't let that put you off. There are tips throughout the method to help you achieve a really beautiful finished quilt. Over the years I've made every mistake in the book so learn from my errors and your patchwork will be the envy of all!

When it comes to quilting there are three options: quilt by hand (a labour of love!) quilt by machine (faster but a whole skill set to master) or quilt by chequebook. Making a quilt is a labour of love but it's worth it . . . Look after your quilt and it will last a lifetime.

YOU WILL NEED:
30CM (12IN) EACH OF TWENTY DIFFERENT FABRICS FOR THE QUILT TOP
MATCHING SEWING THREADS FOR PIECING AND QUILTING
2.3X2.7M (90X108IN) BACKING FABRIC (YOU MIGHT HAVE TO PIECE THIS)
QUILT BASTING SPRAY, SUCH AS 505
2.3X2.7M (90X108IN) QUILT WADDING
68CM (27IN) FABRIC FOR THE QUILT BINDING

FINISHED SIZE: 2X2.5M (80X100IN)

1. Choose three fabrics. From one of them cut one 16cm (6½in) square (A). From the second fabric cut two strips, each 4cm (1½in) wide (B). One of the strips should be the width of the fabric (so approximately 100–110cm/40–42in) and the other should be 35cm (14in). From the third fabric cut two strips each 16cm (6½in) wide (C). One should be the width of the fabric and the other should be 35cm (14in).

Stuart's Tip

Start by making one block; this ensures you understand the pattern and the method, that your cutting and piecing is accurate and that your colour choices please you. You could always make this an extra block and use it for the Quilted Cushion, see page 162. Use accurate 0.5cm (¼in) seams throughout.

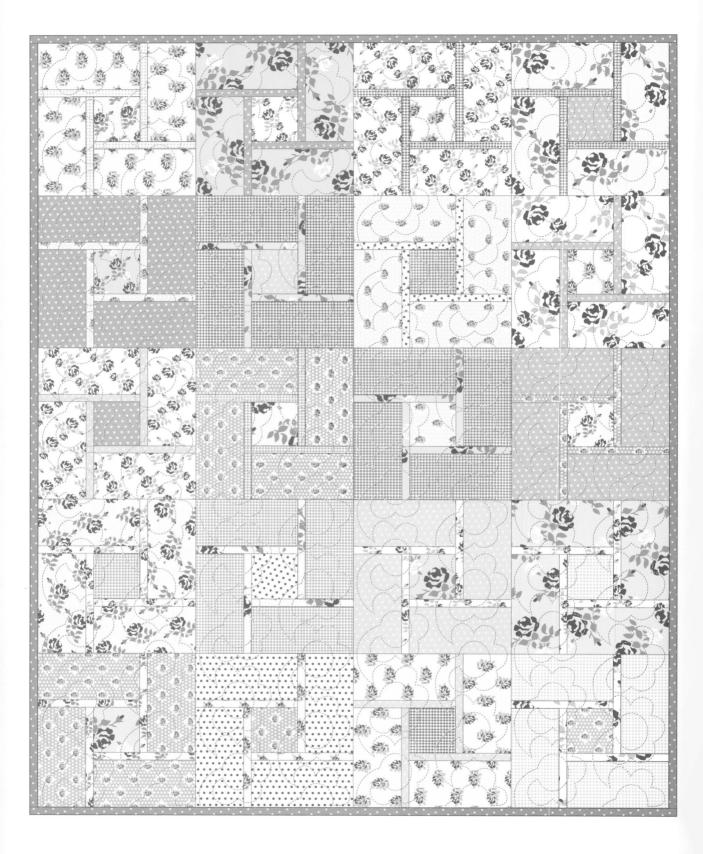

2. Sew long strip B to long strip C. Likewise, sew the 35cm (14in) strips together to make two strip sets. Press the seam allowances towards the wider strips.

3. From the long pieced strip set cut three sections each 34cm (13½in) long. From the 35cm (14in) strip set cut one more 34cm (13½in) section. You should have four sections, each 19x34cm (7½x13½in).

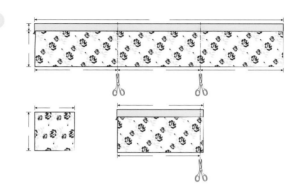

4. Take your 16cm (6½in) square (A) and lay it in front of you, right side up. Lay one of the pieced sections on top of the square, with the raw edges of fabric B matched up with the raw edges of fabric A. Also match the left edges; the right edges of the pieced section are obviously longer . . . don't panic!

5. Pin and then sew the seam. You are going to sew a partial seam. All this means is that you are going to sew about half of this first seam, starting at the left edge (where everything matches up) and stitching about 8cm (3in) along. Press this partial seam allowance towards fabric C.

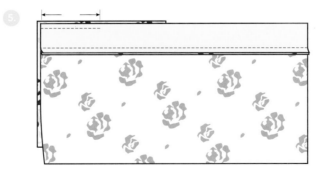

6. Turn your block a quarter-turn clockwise. Add the second pieced unit to this adjacent side, this time you can sew across the whole side. Make sure you pin your patches together for accuracy. Press the seam allowances towards fabric C.

7. Repeat step 6 twice more until you have added all four pieced sections to the centre square.

8. Finally, return to that partial seam. You can now match up the remaining seam and finish stitching it. Press the seam allowance towards fabric C.

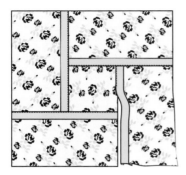

Stuart's Tip

It's a good idea to measure your block from raw edge to raw edge. It should measure 51.5x51.5cm (20½x20½in). If it is bigger then your seam allowances are probably a bit skinny. If your block is smaller than it should be then you are probably sewing with too large a seam allowance. It's worth checking and adjusting your seam allowances now before you make the whole quilt! That way your blocks will fit together easily!

9. Make a total of 20 blocks following steps 1–8. Lay your blocks out on the floor in five rows of four and take a step back. Look at your quilt top; do any blocks jump out at you? If you feel that any of the blocks are not in the right position, change them now. When you are happy with your layout sew the blocks into five rows of four blocks. Press the seam allowances on the first row to the right, on the second row to the left and so on, then sew the five rows together. Your seam intersections should all meet and the seam allowances should be pressed in opposite directions. As always, pin before you sew and make sure your seam allowances are 0.5cm (¼in) and straight.

10. Press your finished quilt top. It should measure 201x251cm (80½x100½in). Lay your backing fabric, wrong side up, on a clean, flat surface. Spray evenly with quilt basting spray. Lay your quilt wadding on top and smooth out any wrinkles; make sure that the surfaces are bonded together well. Spray the wadding with basting spray and then lay your quilt top on top, right side up. The wadding and backing will be several inches bigger on all sides. Smooth out any wrinkles and make sure that the quilt 'sandwich' is bonded well.

Stuart's Tip

If this all seems beyond you, send the finished quilt top to a 'longarm quilter', who will layer your quilt top with wadding and backing and professionally machine quilt it for you (quilting by chequebook – love it!).

11. Time to quilt! Hand quilt with matching thread and a small neat running stitch or use a walking foot on your machine and a stitch length slightly longer than normal to machine sew through all three layers. This 'quilting' will hold the layers together. You should quilt at least along all the block edges and through the centre of each block. The more quilting you add the stronger and more durable your quilt will be.

12. When the quilting is completed, trim the quilt wadding and backing even with the quilt top. The raw edges will be covered with quilt binding. Take your quilt binding fabric and cut ten strips each 6cm (2½in) wide by the width of the fabric. Join them end to end with diagonal seams. Add the binding to your quilt (see Binding a Quilt, page 49.

13. It's a lovely final touch to add a label to the back of your quilt. This can be made plain or fancy but at its simplest it can be made from a plain fabric with a few details about the maker (that's you!) written on with a safe permanent fabric pen or embroidered by hand or machine. Include your name, home town or city, date you finished the quilt and who it was made for.

PROJECT VARIATIONS

Use the same block to make quilts in many different sizes:

- *Just one block makes a perfect 50cm (20in) square quilted cushion (see Quilted Cushion, page 162).*

- *Make four blocks in pretty pastels or novelty prints for a baby quilt measuring 1x1m (40x40in).*

- *Nine blocks make a perfect picnic blanket that measures 150cm (60in) square. You could back this quilt with laminated cotton to avoid soggy bottoms!*

- *Twelve blocks in a four by three layout will make a quilt that finishes 150x200cm (60x80in); great for a single bed.*

- *Twenty-five blocks set in a five by five layout will make a quilt that is 2.5m (100in) square, perfect for a king size bed.*

- *The centre square A is the perfect place for highlighting a special motif in your fabric or for showcasing embroideries or appliqués.*

Stuart's Story

I made my first patchwork quilt when I was twenty-one years old. It seemed like the natural thing to do with a pile of scrap fabrics, and with no more than a cardboard template and a pair of blunt kitchen scissors, I started hacking at them. I cut and sewed through the night until my fingers were sore and I heard the milkman delivering his round. I had already learned some important facts on my very first day:

1. Scissors give you blisters – use a rotary cutter instead.

2. Quilting is obsessive behaviour and it can take over your life!

That first quilt turned out pretty lumpy and misshapen – the seams frayed and the top rippled like the surface of the moon – but I didn't care. I loved that quilt and I used it till it fell apart many years later. That love affair with fabric, and with quilts in particular, has never waned. Despite the odd gaff, the mismatched fabrics and squares that refused to meet at 90 degrees, I have never made a quilt I didn't adore because I love the process so much.

Quilts mean many things to the people who make them and to those who receive them. Some quilts tell a story in the shapes and scenes appliquéd to them; others are a travelogue of the places where the fabrics were bought or the people who wore them; and then there are those that are no more or less than a celebration of beautiful fabric and the love that goes into every stitch.

Whatever reason you choose to quilt, I hope you adore the process and the end result as much as I do.

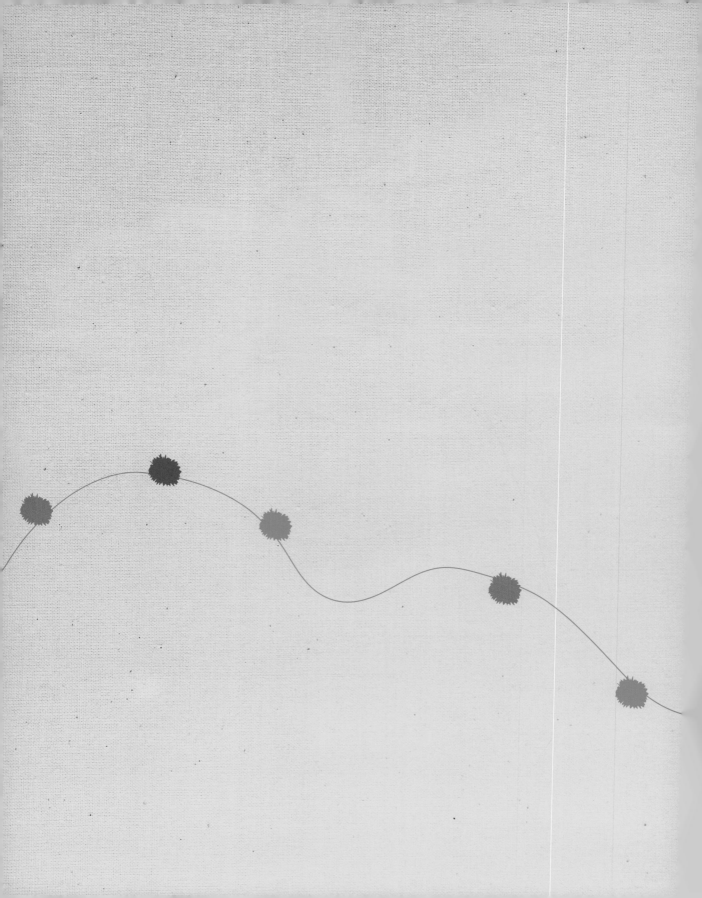

GARDEN GRACES
RETRO

There is nothing more wonderful than relaxing in a well-kept, colourful garden; trouble is, I don't come close to possessing a green thumb. I do try but I just don't have the resilience to go out in all winds and weathers to keep up the maintenance. To solve this seemingly impossible demand I have filled my garden with shrubs and greenery so hardy it could withstand a nuclear winter and I bring instant colour and cheer to this emerald canvas with sewn fabric garden accessories. The vibrant deckchairs, windmills and beanbag chairs in this chapter don't need nurturing to blossom brightly. The bunting is quite happy to accept my thoughtless neglect and when I'm entertaining, my huge picnic quilt and plump floor cushions hide the shabbiest of lawns. Whether you are a first rate gardener or a bit of a fair weather horticulturist like me, your garden can be the envy of your neighbours, you simply need to sew.

Garden Windmills 176

Bunting 178

Beanbag Lounger 182

Revamped Deckchair 185

Picnic Set including Place Mat, Cutlery Roll and Napkins 190

Garden Quilt 194

GARDEN WINDMILLS

Childhood holidays on the bracing coast were the inspiration for these simple windmills. Bravely battling the wind was transformed from chore to joy when one of these whirling delights was shoved into my pudgy hand. Whether you take them to the beach or plant them in the flowerbeds, they are sure to bring colour and joy!

YOU WILL NEED:
PAINTED WOODEN DOWEL, APPROXIMATELY 30–35CM (12–14IN) LONG AND 1CM (½IN) IN DIAMETER
4CM (1½IN) THIN NAIL
CONTRASTING FABRICS FOR BOTH SIDES OF THE WINDMILL
DOUBLE-SIDED HEAVYWEIGHT FUSIBLE INTERFACING, SUCH AS FAST2FUSE
HOLE PUNCH OR 5.5CM (¼IN) EYELET KIT
HOT GLUE GUN
DECORATIVE BUTTON

1. Knock the nail into the dowel, about 2.5cm (1in) from the top.

2. Cut out one 20cm (8in) square from each fabric and mark the centre on one of the squares lightly with a pencil. Cut one square of fusible interfacing to the same size and, following the manufacturer's instructions, fuse the fabric squares to either side of the interfacing.

3. Cut diagonal lines from each corner towards the centre, stopping 5cm (2in) from the centre point. Use your hole punch to cut a hole in the very centre of the square and at each corner, about 1cm (½in) in from the tip. If you prefer, use a 5.5cm (¼ in) eyelet kit to put eyelets in the centre and at the four corner marks.

4. Fold each tip towards the centre hole, line them all up then pass the thin nail through the holes/eyelets.

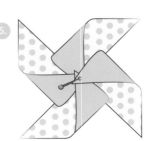

5. Glue a decorative button to the head of the nail to hold the sails of the windmill in place, making sure they can still turn.

MEDIUM

BUNTING

Beautiful, brightly coloured bunting lends a suitably carnival atmosphere to the garden.
These fluttering fabric pennants do not need to be reserved for parties, pin them to fences
and between trees to celebrate those wonderfully rare sunny days!

YOU WILL NEED:
ASSORTED SCRAPS OF BRIGHTLY COLOURED FABRICS, EACH 18X23CM (7X9IN)
BUNTING TRIANGLE, SEE TEMPLATES ON PAGE 56, CUT OUT IN CARD OR
TEMPLATE PLASTIC
MATCHING SEWING THREAD
1CM (½IN) WIDE BIAS BINDING (TRY MAKING YOUR OWN, SEE STEP 6)
FINISHED SIZE: EACH PENNANT IS 15X20CM (6X8IN)

1.   Place two matching or contrasting fabrics right sides together and pin in
     place. Draw around your bunting triangle on the wrong side of one fabric.

2.   Sew along the line down the two long sides only. Backstitch at the
     beginning and end of your line of stitching to secure.

3.   Trim the fabric to within 0.5cm (¼in) of your marked line on all three
     sides. Trim off the seam allowance at the point very close to the
     stitching line.

4.   Turn the triangle through to the right side and push out the point with a
     point turner or chopstick. Press the triangle flat.

5.   Make as many triangles as you require. For each metre (yard) of bunting
     you will need approximately five finished triangles.

6.   If you are making your own binding cut strips of fabric on the straight
     of grain, each 5cm (2in) wide. Join the strips end to end to the required
     length then fold the strip in half and then the raw edges towards the
     centre fold to make binding that is about 1cm (½in) wide.

7. Leaving a few inches of binding spare at the start, carefully sandwich a bunting triangle inside the fold of the binding and pin in place. Leave a gap of about 2.5cm (1in) and then repeat. Keep going like this until you have used up all your triangles or binding.

8. Using a sewing machine carefully sew along the bottom edge of the binding strip to hold all the bunting triangles in place. Sew about 3mm (⅛in) from the lower edge, making sure you catch both sides of the binding.

PROJECT VARIATIONS:

- *Use patterned fabric on one side, plain on the other.*

- *Add bobble trim to the outside of each triangle.*

- *Add fusible appliqués to the bunting triangles to spell out a name, 'Happy Birthday' or 'Congratulations'.*

- *This bunting doesn't have to stay outside. Make it in colours to match your bedroom, nursery, bathroom or kitchen and bring the party indoors!*

BEANBAG LOUNGER

A huge, squishy, chair-shaped lounger for long sessions of reading in the garden, snoozing under trees or general lazy sprawling. So comfy you may never want to move again!

YOU WILL NEED:
1M (40IN) FABRIC FOR THE BEANBAG CHAIR SIDES
MATCHING SEWING THREAD
BEANBAG PATTERN PIECE A (SEE PAGE 56)
3M (3¼YD) CONTRAST FABRIC FOR THE SEAT, BACK AND BASE OF THE LOUNGER
65CM (26IN) ZIP
3M (3¼YD) CALICO, 140CM (54IN) WIDE
LARGE BAG OF POLYSTYRENE BEANBAG FILLING

FINISHED SIZE: TO SUIT ONE ADULT

1. Start by making the outer lounger first. Fold your 1m (40in) piece of fabric in half, right sides together and cut two pieces of fabric for the lounger sides using pattern piece A. You will have one piece for the left and the reverse for the right.

2. From the 3m (3¼yd) piece of contrast fabric cut a strip on the lengthwise grain that is 295x67.5cm (118x27in) to make the welt. Press under 1cm (½in) at either short end. Unfold this hem and pin the fabric, right sides together, into a circle. Sew along this seam for the first and last 2.5cm (1in) only, using a 1cm (½in) seam allowance. The 62.5cm (25in) that is unsewn in the centre is for the zip.

3. Centre the zip on the back of the seam and pin in place. Sew the zip into place (see Inserting a Zip, page 44). Undo the first 5–8cm (2–3in) of the zip.

4. Pin one side of this circle to one of the side pieces. Position the zip at the bottom of the back as indicated on the pattern piece. Use lots of pins and ease the welt around the curved sides. Sew the first side using a 1cm (½in) seam allowance, take it steady around the curves and remove the pins as you go. Join the other side in exactly the same way as the first.

5. Undo the zip fully and turn the beanbag cover through to the right side.

6. Make the inner calico lining in exactly the same way – there is no zip to insert but you still need to leave the centre 62.5cm (25in) unsewn to fill the bag with beans.

7. Half fill the calico lining with polystyrene beanbag filling. Be really careful doing this as the filling has a tendency to fly everywhere and could quickly turn your living room into a winter wonderland! Don't be tempted to overfill at this stage or you will never get the liner into the outer cover! Place the half filled calico inner inside the fabric outer and continue to fill the calico lining with the filling. Again, don't overfill the lining as you need to leave some space for the pellets to move around!

8. When you have finished filling the calico lining pin the gap closed and hand sew firmly using a ladder stitch.

9. Close the zip on the outer cover and lounge!

PROJECT VARIATION

You can add covered piping cord to the sides if you like; this will add a decorative touch and make the seams more durable. You will need to make 6.5m (7yd) of covered piping cord to do this.

REVAMPED DECKCHAIR

There was a time when every British coastal resort would have been jam-packed with row upon row of striped canvas chairs and before they hit the beaches these fantastic folding chairs were a common sight on liners and cruise ships. Look in your garden shed and you may well find a couple of these beach babes hiding under the compost just waiting for a glamorous makeover. Grab deckchair canvas, upholstery tacks, a hammer and some jumbo bobble trim and you'll be wedged in that revamped lounger before you can say 'kiss me quick'! And if you want to take it one step further, you can make a headrest and attached holdall to match (see page 188).

YOU WILL NEED:

OLD DECKCHAIR IN NEED OF TLC (CANVAS AND TACKS REMOVED) OR A NEW FRAME

140CM (54IN) DECKCHAIR CANVAS; CHOOSE THE BRIGHTEST STRIPES YOUR EYEBALLS CAN TOLERATE!

UPHOLSTERY TACKS

SMALL HAMMER

JUMBO BOBBLE TRIM OR TASSEL TRIM (OPTIONAL)

1. Lay your deckchair canvas out on a large flat surface to work on – the floor works for me! Turn your deckchair upside down and erect it. This gets the frame out of your way and makes putting new canvas on much easier. You want the head end nearest you.

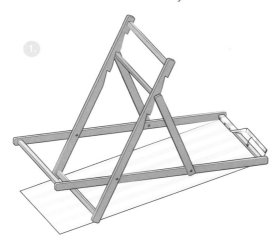

2. Take the canvas over the top bar and fold under a 2.5cm (1in) hem to neaten the raw edge. The stripes on the canvas make it virtually impossible to do this badly – just line up the stripes and it'll be perfect! Now position the fold on the lower edge of the head rail and hammer an upholstery tack right in the centre. There's a certain knack to holding the tack between two fingers and banging it in straight. If the tack bends or breaks just lever it out and try again.

3. Add tacks at either side, then a couple more between each of those tacks. Approximately nine tacks should do it.

4. Go to the foot end of the chair. Pull the canvas taut; you'll probably have a little too much canvas, so trim off the excess, leaving enough to wrap around the foot bar with a hem added. The bar at the foot end is narrower than the canvas so fold the sides of your canvas in by 2.5cm (1in) and wrap it around the wooden bar. Tuck under a neat hem and repeat the tacking process. Again, nine tacks should be plenty.

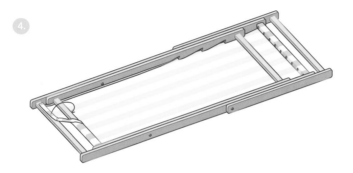

5. You could leave your deckchair revamp there – it will stay looking fabulous so long as you remember to bring it inside every night. Deckchair canvas will fade so to keep your chairs looking their best, re-cover every spring!

PROJECT VARIATION

I added jumbo bobble trim to the front edge of the foot end wooden bar. To do the same, just cut to size, position and nail in place with upholstery tacks. You could even use a glue gun for this stage as the trim is purely decorative.

MEDIUM

OPTIONAL HEADREST AND HOLDALL

Add extra comfort by making this squishy headrest. There's also a handy holdall hanging off the back to store sunblock, a book and water bottle. Deckchair canvas has a firmly woven selvedge so it can be sewn on the right side and still looks neat and tidy.

YOU WILL NEED:
1.8M (2YD) DECKCHAIR CANVAS
40X30CM (16X12IN) CUSHION PAD
MATCHING SEWING THREAD
JUMBO BOBBLE TRIM (OPTIONAL)
UPHOLSTERY TACKS

1. Starting at one end of your canvas, place the cushion pad on top and wrap the canvas around it. You don't want it tightly bound, so give the pad a bit of room to breathe. Fold the raw edge under by 2.5cm (1in) and crease along the fold. Pin in place and then remove the cushion pad.

2. Sew across the pinned edge and also down one side. Snip off any thread ends to neaten.

3. Re-insert the cushion pad through the side opening, squish the pillow down and sew the open edge together again, using your sewing machine. Turn the canvas over so the turned/sewn hem is on the bottom.

4. For the hanging pocket, turn the top raw edge down by 10cm (4in) and press. Turn the raw edge under by 5cm (2in) and insert a piece of jumbo bobble trim under this edge if you want. Sew the edge. Fold this trimmed/hemmed edge up by 40cm (16in) to make the hanging pocket, then pin and sew the side seams.

5. Hang the pillow/pocket over the top rail of the deckchair. The weight of the pillow is enough to hold everything in place but if you want it secured just hammer in a row of five or seven upholstery tacks.

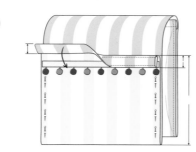

PICNIC SET INCLUDING PLACE MAT, CUTLERY ROLL AND NAPKINS

I love eating in the garden and will do so whenever the weather allows. Likewise, I will go for a picnic at the drop of a (sun) hat and these picnic place mat, cutlery roll and napkin sets take outdoor dining to a whole new level! I keep a couple of these combos in the glove compartment of my car for when I'm on the road and am reduced to eating a takeaway in a parking lot. Standards have to be maintained!

YOU WILL NEED:
50X32.5CM (20X13IN) INNER FABRIC (A)
MATCHING SEWING THREADS
23CM (9IN) SQUARE ACCENT FABRIC (C)
TWO 5X23CM (2X13IN) STRIPS ACCENT FABRIC (C)
50X32.5CM (20X13IN) QUILT WADDING
50X32.5CM (20X13IN) OUTER FABRIC (B)
50CM (20IN) SQUARE NAPKIN FABRIC (D)

1. Lay the inner fabric rectangle (A) out in front of you with the long edges at the top and bottom.

2. Fold the accent fabric square (C) in half on the diagonal, wrong sides together, and topstitch a couple of lines along the folded edge: the first 0.5cm (¼in) from the folded edge and the second 1cm (½in) from the edge. Place this piece on top of rectangle A on the bottom left corner, matching the outer raw edges. Pin or baste in place. Now sew vertical lines from the folded edge of the triangle down to the raw outer edge at 5cm (2in) and 11cm (4½in) in from the left to make channels for your cutlery.

3. Take one of the fabric strips (C) and fold in half lengthwise, wrong sides together, and press. Fold the raw edges in towards the centre and press again, then fold one short end in twice to neaten and topstitch across this short edge and down the folded edge. Repeat to make two ties.

4. Lay these two ties in the middle of the right short end rectangle A with the raw short edges aligned with the raw edges of rectangle (see illustration). Lay the rectangle of wadding on top and finally lay the outer fabric rectangle (B) on top, right side down. Pin all the layers together.

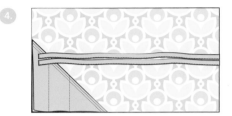 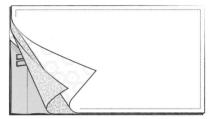

5. Sew around the perimeter of the rectangle with a 1cm (½in) seam allowance. Leave a gap of approximately 8cm (3in) in the centre of one long edge for turning through.

6. Clip off the seam allowance at the corners close to the stitching line to reduce the bulk. Turn through to the right side and push out the corners with a point turner or chopstick.

7. Slip stitch the opening closed by hand then topstitch around the perimeter of the roll, 0.5cm (¼in) from the edge.

8. To make the napkin turn in a 0.5cm (¼in) hem on all four sides of your napkin square (D) and repeat to enclose the raw edges. Topstitch close to the folded edge.

PROJECT VARIATIONS

- *Vary the inner and outer fabrics with designs from the same range to create a coordinated look that isn't too 'samey'.*

- *Increase the size of the roll and instead of a folded triangle use a long folded square and stitch channels at 2.5cm (1in) intervals to create a handy storage roll for knitting needles, crochet hooks, artists' paintbrushes or coloured pencils.*

GARDEN QUILT

A gloriously big quilt for lounging on in the garden and it would also work wonderfully in a modern bright boudoir. The pattern is the same as the bedroom Patchwork Quilt (see page 165). However, for this quilt, a smaller range of fabrics have been used as well as a unifying block centre and plain white fabric, which alter the look dramatically.

YOU WILL NEED:

45CM (18IN) OF EACH OF TEN DIFFERENT FABRICS IN BRIGHT ORANGES AND PINKS

MATCHING THREADS FOR PIECING AND QUILTING

115CM (45IN) PLAIN WHITE FABRIC FOR THE BLOCKS

67.5CM (27IN) BRIGHT PINK AND ORANGE POLKA DOT FABRIC FOR THE BLOCK CENTRES

2.3X2.7M (90X108IN) QUILT WADDING

QUILT BASTING SPRAY, SUCH AS 505

2.3X2.7M (90X108IN) QUILT BACKING FABRIC (YOU MAY NEED TO PIECE THIS)

67.5CM (27IN) FABRIC FOR THE BINDING

FINISHED SIZE: 2X2.5M (80X100IN)

1. Follow the instructions for the bedroom Patchwork Quilt (see page 165). You need two blocks from each of the ten fabrics so you will need to cut two strips, each 16cm (6½in) by width of fabric. From your plain white fabric cut a total of twenty 4cm (1½in) by width of fabric strips and from the pink and orange polka dot cut a total of twenty 16cm (6½in) squares for the block centres.

2. Make twenty blocks in total and then join them in a four by five arrangement.

3. Layer the top with wadding and backing fabric, baste and machine quilt or have your top professionally quilted by a longarm quilter.

4. Bind the quilt with ten strips of binding fabric cut 6cm (2½in) wide and joined end to end. Don't forget to add a label to the back of your quilt.

Stuart's Tip

Remember, if you still want to make a gorgeous quilt but would rather spend time sunbathing on it than making it, send the finished quilt top to a 'longarm quilter', who will layer your quilt top with wadding and backing and professionally machine quilt it for you.

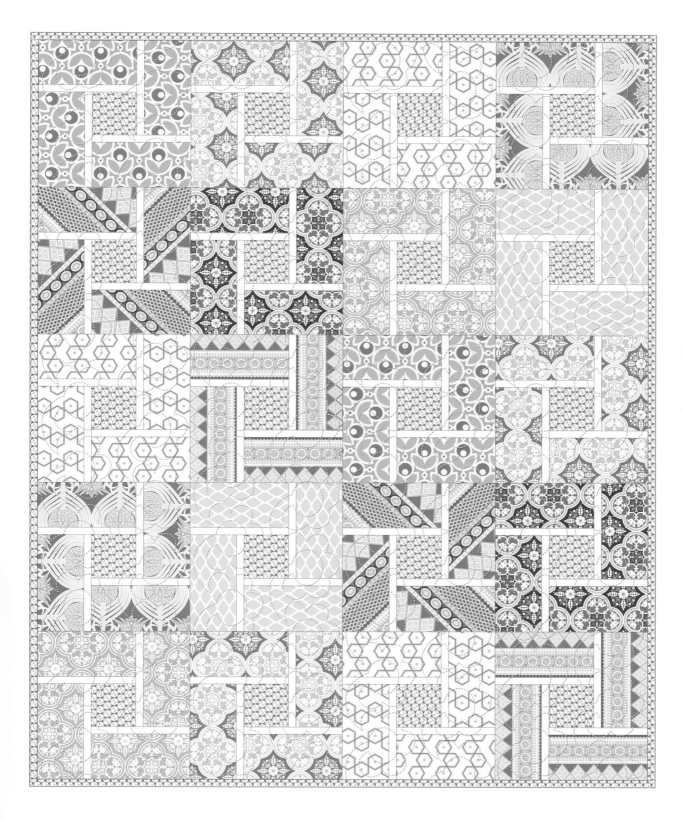

GORGEOUS GIFTS

Home-sewn gifts have a very special appeal; they are unique, can be personalised to fit the recipients personality and they show your thoughtfulness like a bought gift never could! Cushions and quilts, aprons and bags, napkins and embellished towels all make great gifts but in this chapter you'll find a few other projects that are perfect for making and giving. When a gift has been handmade it doesn't matter whether your sewing is perfect or not, your time and love will be there forever – in every stitch!

Scented Scrap Heart 202

Splash-proof Gadget Covers 204

Men's Gadget or Wash Bag 206

Beauty Bag 208

Sun Hat 212

Beach Poncho 214

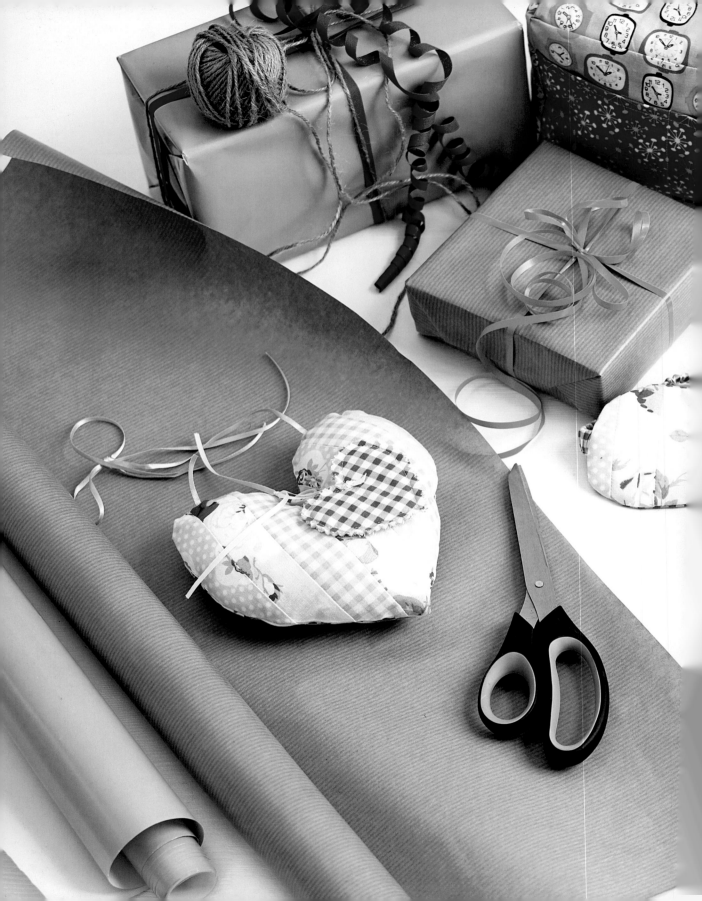

PERSONALISING YOUR GIFTS

Gorgeous gifts don't need to cost a fortune to be treasured forever. In this chapter, I've included an array of small and easy-to-make gift items that will appeal to men, women and children of all ages. None of them take very long to make and all can be personalised. Nothing says 'I made this for you' like a bit of personalisation.

You can personalise them with quickly fused appliqués (see Fusible Appliqué, page 34) and add a monogram, initials of a name, 'Mr and Mrs', anything at all! I also made embroidered luggage labels for my 'His' and 'Hers' bags (see photo, page 208). Machine embroidered labels are easy to make and can be transferred from one bag to the next. To make an embroidered label:

1. Print or photocopy the name or word and then trace it onto the right side of a piece of plain fabric. Cut the fabric bigger than the finished size so it's easier to handle.

2. Fuse the fabric to a piece of stiff interfacing.

3. Add another piece of plain or patterned fabric on the reverse, pretty side out.

4. Set your sewing machine for a straight stitch, a shorter stitch length than normal, and the same colour in the top and bobbin. Stitch over your drawn letters several times until you have a density that pleases you. If you attach the darning foot on your sewing machine you can 'scribble' along the traced lines which is easier! Clip your loose threads off when you've finished.

5. Cut the name out allowing a 1cm (½in) border all around, then clip the corners off one end so it looks like a luggage tag.

6. Add a grommet at one end following the manufacturers instructions.

7. Thread ribbon through the grommet and attach your tag to your gift.

8. Voila!

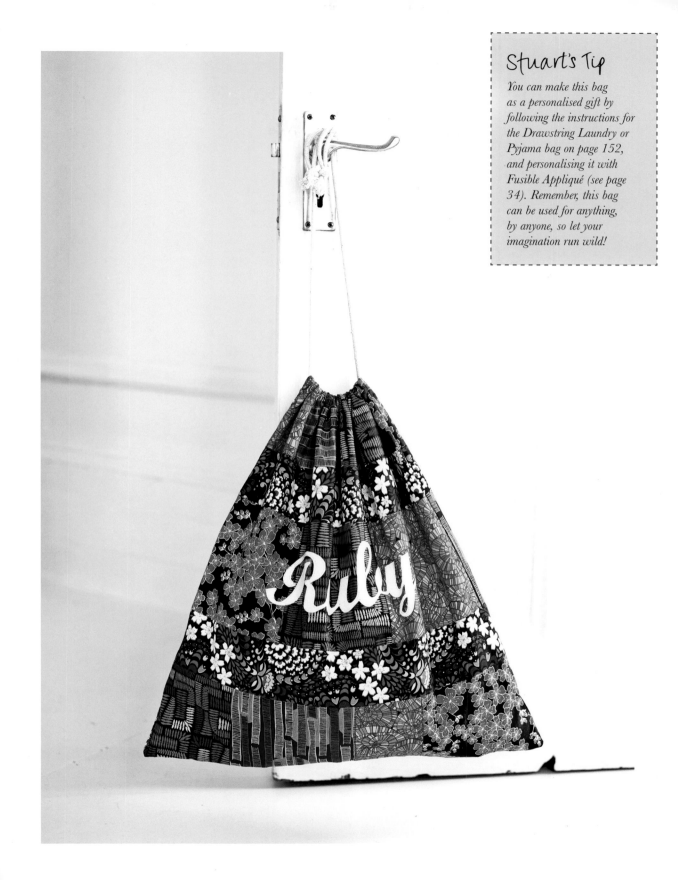

Stuart's Tip

You can make this bag as a personalised gift by following the instructions for the Drawstring Laundry or Pyjama bag on page 152, and personalising it with Fusible Appliqué (see page 34). Remember, this bag can be used for anything, by anyone, so let your imagination run wild!

EASY

SCENTED SCRAP HEART

This pretty heart uses up small scraps and can be stuffed with lavender or fine potpourri to scent your boudoir, or filled with wheat and used as a little hottie. Who wouldn't want a warm heart?

YOU WILL NEED:

SCRAPS OF VARIOUS COTTON FABRICS, ALL 4CM (1½IN) WIDE AND AT LEAST 18CM (7IN) LONG

MATCHING SEWING THREAD

20CM (8IN) SQUARE OF BACKING FABRIC

90CM (36IN) FINE RIBBON

HEART TEMPLATE (SEE PAGE 56), CUT OUT OF TISSUE PAPER

POLYESTER FIBREFILL FOR STUFFING OR APPROXIMATELY 2 CUPS OF DRIED LAVENDER, FINE POTPOURRI OR WHEAT

FINISHED SIZE: 18X16CM (7X6½IN)

1. Sew enough scraps together to make a piece of patchwork fabric approximately 20x20cm (8x8in). Press all your seam allowances neatly.

2. Cut your 20cm (8in) square of backing fabric in half and then sew the two pieces back together, with a 1cm (½in) seam allowance and leaving a 5cm (2in) opening in the middle.

3. Cut the ribbon in half. Lay your patchwork fabric in front of you, right sides up, next lay your ribbon pieces on top with one raw end from each piece at the top and the rest of the ribbon in the centre of your patchwork fabric. Now lay your backing piece on top, right side down, with the gap for turning in the middle. Place the heart template on top and pin through all the layers.

4. Sew all around the outside of the heart. Remove the template, trim the excess fabric leaving a 0.5cm (¼in) seam allowance and clip down to but not through the seam allowance at the inward point of the heart. Turn the heart through to the right side. Stuff the heart firmly with fibrefill of fill with lavender, potpourri or wheat. Slip stitch the opening closed.

5. If you used wheat to fill your heart you can heat the heart by placing it on a microwaveable plate and microwaving on full power for 1–2 minutes. A drop or two of lavender or rose geranium essential oil on the heart will guarantee a sweet fragrance!

SPLASH-PROOF GADGET COVERS

Make these covers for your e-book, real book(!), phone, tablet or laptop in splash-proof cotton laminate or oilcloth. They are super fast and easy and close with stick-on Velcro. It doesn't get much easier than this!

YOU WILL NEED:

OILCLOTH OR LAMINATED COTTON CUT TO SIZE (SEE ESTIMATING FABRIC BOX)
PAPER CLIPS
MATCHING SEWING THREAD
SELF-ADHESIVE HOOK-AND-LOOP TAPE, SUCH AS VELCRO, 2CM (¾IN) WIDE AND HALF THE WIDTH OF YOUR DEVICE

1. Cut the piece of oilcloth or laminate to size. Fold it around your device so that there is an overlap at the top, one-third of the depth of your device or book. Remove the book or device. Hold the side seams in place with the paper clips.

2. Sew the side seams. I use a walking foot on my machine to make the sewing easier. Do the same if you have one.

3. Stick one half of the Velcro in the middle of the front flap, on the wrong side and the remaining piece of Velcro on the right side under the flap.

ESTIMATING FABRIC

*   *To calculate the length: start at the top of your book or device, measure down to the bottom, under the bottom, back up to the top and then down the front again, a third of the way from the top.*

*   *To calculate the width: measure from the centre of one side of your fabric to the centre of the other and add on 5cm (2in).*

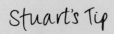

Stuart's Tip

Use a saucer or plate to mark the front flap into a curve. Sticky Velcro dots work better for the fastening if you shape the front flap.

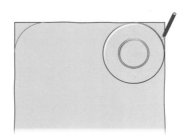

MEDIUM

MEN'S GADGET OR WASH BAG

This handy drawstring bag is so useful you won't stop at one! In the bathroom I've lined my bag with laminated cotton in case any of the contents are a little damp, making it ideal for a shaving kit or wash bag. The cord lock or toggle stops the contents falling out in transit.

YOU WILL NEED:
25CM (10IN) FABRIC FOR THE OUTER BAG
25CM (10IN) LAMINATED COTTON FOR THE LINING
50CM (20IN) CORD FOR THE DRAWSTRING
CORD LOCK/TOGGLE

FINISHED SIZE: 23X28CM (9X11IN)

1. From the outer fabric cut two panels, each 25x32.5cm (10x13in). Cut two panels from the lining fabric to the same dimensions.

2. To make the bag outer take the two outer fabric panels and place them right sides together. Measure 4cm (1½in) down from the top and place a pin at both sides of the top. Sew from this mark down to one corner, across the bottom then up the other side until you reach the pin. Remove the pins and press the seam allowances open. Fold the seam allowance back for the final unsewn 4cm (1½in) at both sides of the top, press and topstitch around this 'V'. Fold the bag in half so that the side seams are centred in the middle. Measure 4cm (1½in) in from the bottom corner on each side and mark a line across the corner. Sew along this line and cut the corners off; this makes the bottom of the bag more 'squared off', it's more practical too.

3. Make the lining in exactly the same way.

4. Turn the outer bag and lining bag right sides out and place the lining inside so the wrong sides are together. Match the tops and sew a line 0.5cm (¼in) from the top edge to attach the lining to the outer bag. Turn the raw edge down 1cm (½ in), then turn it down to the bottom of the 'V' to make the casing. Pin in place then stitch all around the casing.

5. Attach a safety pin to the cord and thread it through the casing. Remove the safety pin and thread both ends of cord through the cord lock. Knot the ends of the cord and trim to 0.5cm (¼in).

PROJECT VARIATIONS

- *This bag works brilliantly for storing toiletries or hairbrushes in your handbag, but I would still use a laminate for the lining just in case.*

- *Lined in regular cotton or even unlined (overlock or zigzag stitch the seam if you are not lining it), this bag is great for all kinds of gadgets. I've made one for every different charging unit I possess and added fabric labels to the bags to remind me which one is which!*

- *Halve the width and reduce the length to 20cm (8in) to make a perfect little bag for sunglasses and spectacles. Don't forget to add seam allowances to those dimensions! Why not appliqué a pair of specs, cut out in fusible-backed fabric, to the front panel of the bag?*

BEAUTY BAG

I wouldn't say no to a bag like this so don't think it is just for the girls. There's plenty of room for toiletries and Lord knows, the older I get the more products it takes. Use 1cm (½in) seam allowances throughout.

YOU WILL NEED:
45CM (18IN) FABRIC FOR THE OUTER BAG
45CM (18IN) FABRIC FOR THE BAG LINING (LAMINATED COTTON WILL MAKE THE INSIDE OF THE BAG WIPE CLEAN)
90CM (36IN) LIGHTWEIGHT FUSIBLE INTERFACING
MATCHING SEWING THREADS
18CM (7IN) ZIP

FINISHED SIZE: 20X12.5X10CM (8X5X4IN)

1. Cut two pieces from the outer bag fabric, each 23x15cm (9x6in); these will be the front and back panels. Now cut two more pieces, each 23x23cm (9x9in); these are for the pocket panels. Finally cut a piece that is 55x12.5cm (22x5in) for the welt and two zip band sections, each 23x8cm (9x3in).

2. Cut exactly the same pieces from the lining fabric.

3. Cut out the same pieces from the iron-on lightweight interfacing, including two extra pocket panels. Interface all of the lining fabric pieces and the two outer pocket panels.

4. To make the outer pockets, fold one of the interfaced outer pocket panels in half to make a pocket that measures 23x11cm (9x4½in). Repeat the step to make two.

5. Align the raw edges of the folded pockets with the bottom of the bag front panel; the folded edge of the pocket, which forms the top, should be 4cm (1½in) from the bag front top. Baste in place around the sides and bottom. Stitch a line up the centre of the pocket to divide it into two. Repeat to add a pocket to the back panel.

6. Make the zip band: press a 1cm (½in) hem down one long edge of each zip band section. Stitch the two zip band pieces together, just 2.5cm (1in) along this fold; leave the centre 18cm (7in) unstitched then sew the remaining 2.5cm (1in). Press the seam allowance open, centre your 18cm (7in) zip and stitch in place (see Inserting a Zip, page 44).

7. Join the zip band to the bag welt at both short ends to make a ring. With right sides together and the zip band section running along the top of the band, pin and join the zip band to the bag front. Clip into your seam allowances where necessary to ensure a smooth fit. Join the bag back to the other side of the zip band/welt.

8. The bag lining is made in exactly the same way as the bag outer; make the inner pockets first and baste them to the bag lining fronts, join the zip band at either end but don't insert a zip this time! Join the welt and zip bands then sew the welt/band to the lining fronts.

9. Turn the bag outer wrong sides out and the lining right sides out. Slip the lining over the bag outer so that the wrong sides are touching each other. Slip stitch by hand around the zip to join the outer to the lining. Turn the bag right sides out.

10. Fill your bag with stuff!

Stuart's Tip

Don't restrict yourself to the bathroom with this bag; it would be great for carrying craft stuff or to use as a little sewing bag, so make a few and share the love!

SUN HAT

Keep young skin protected with this sweet sun hat. I've used a bright magenta and orange polka dot print with contrast orange lining and a simple bow trim. Any light- to medium-weight cotton or linen fabric would work well and this style suits both boys and girls. You can enlarge or reduce the pattern pieces on a photocopier to adapt the pattern for younger or older children or even for an adult . . . the technique remains the same! Use 1cm (½in) seam allowances throughout.

YOU WILL NEED:
30CM (12IN) COTTON OR LINEN FABRIC (105CM/42IN WIDE) FOR THE OUTER PART OF THE HAT
30CM (12IN) FABRIC FOR THE LINING AND BOW TRIM
23CM (9IN) IRON-ON INTERFACING FOR THE BRIM
MATCHING SEWING THREAD
PATTERN PIECES A (CROWN) B (SIDE) AND C (BRIM) (SEE PAGE 56)

FINISHED SIZE: TO FIT AN AVERAGE SIX-YEAR-OLD (52.5CM/21IN INSIDE CROWN)

1. From the outer fabric cut one crown (A), two sides (B) and two brims (C).

2. Cut the same from the lining fabric, as well as one strip that is 4x50cm (1½x20in) for the bow trim.

3. From the interfacing cut two brims (C). Interface the two brim lining pieces.

4. Sew the two outer hat sides together to form a ring. Press the seam allowances open. Pin the crown to the top of the side pieces matching the notches and sew together. Press the seam allowances towards the side pieces and topstitch close to the seam.

5. Repeat step 4 with the lining pieces.

6. Sew the brim outer pieces together to form a ring; repeat with the interfaced lining brim pieces.

7. Place the brim outer and interfaced brim lining together, right sides together and with top and bottom raw edges matching. Sew the bottom raw edges together, trim to 3mm (⅛in), then turn the brim to the right side. Topstitch at 0.5cm (¼in) intervals from the lower to the upper brim edges.

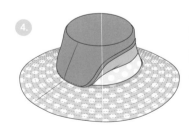

8. Stitch the brim to the hat outer with right sides together; turn the hat wrong side out. Take the crown lining and turn under a 1cm (½in) hem on the bottom edge. Place on top of the hat, wrong sides together, and slip stitch the crown lining in place. You could topstitch from the right side if you prefer.

9. Fold the bow trim strip in half lengthwise and press, turn the raw edges in to the centre and press again to make a folded strip that is 1cm (½in) wide. Topstitch down the long edge, close to the fold. I have knotted the raw ends of the bow trim and tied a bow. This is a casual hat and so I left the ends raw but you could fold them under and stitch if you prefer a more clean look. Stitch the bow to the side of the outer hat.

PROJECT VARIATIONS

• *Make the crown and brim from different fabrics.*

• *Sandwich ric rac between the lower edges of the brim before you sew them together.*

• *Leave off the bow trim altogether or substitute a fabric flower, group of buttons or buckle.*

MEDIUM

BEACH PONCHO

This towelling and fabric poncho is a great way to get kids dry on the beach or when they get out of the pool. It also works as a cover-up when temperatures drop but they still want to play! The poncho has two funky fabrics for the outer with a contrast neck trim and shoulder ties. A pocket has been added to keep a sun hat handy or (more likely) to be filled with beach found 'treasures'. Use 1cm (½in) seams throughout.

YOU WILL NEED:
90CM (36IN) EACH OF TWO DIFFERENT COTTON FABRICS FOR THE OUTER PONCHO
MATCHING SEWING THREADS
90CM (36IN) TOWELLING FABRIC, 150CM (60IN) WIDE, FOR THE INNER PONCHO
2 FAT QUARTERS OF COORDINATING COTTON FABRICS, ONE FOR THE POCKET AND
ONE FOR THE POCKET TRIM AND SHOULDER TIES

**FINISHED SIZE: 71CM (28IN) LONG, FROM SHOULDER TO HEM, AND 89CM
(35IN) WIDE**

1. From each of the two cotton fabrics cut a panel that is 90x75cm (36x30in) and join them together to make a panel measuring 90x148cm (36x59in). Press the seam allowance open.

1. Cut a panel from the towelling that is 90x148cm (36x59in). Lay the joined cotton panel on top of the towel, right sides together, and pin around the edge.

2. Use a small plate or large saucer to round off the four corners, move the pins at the corners to allow you to do this.

3. Sew around the perimeter of the poncho and trim off the excess fabric at the curved corners about 1cm (½in) away from the sewing line.

4. Use the same plate or saucer to draw round and cut the neckline in the centre of the poncho. Turn the poncho through to the right side and press. Topstitch around the outside edge of the poncho 1cm (½in) away from the edge. Also topstitch 1cm (½in) away from each side of the shoulder seam to secure the towelling backing to the fabric front.

5. Bind the neck edge with ready-made bias binding or make your own using 6cm (2½in) wide strips of fabric (see Machine Sewn Binding, page 48).

6. Cut a pocket from one of the contrast fat quarters. This should be cut 28x18cm (11x7in). Then cut a pocket trim that is 28x10cm (11x4in).

7. Sew the trim to the top of the pocket using a 1cm (½in) seam allowance. Press the top edge of the trim down by 1cm (½in) twice and press, then fold it down to cover the join between the main pocket and the trim. Topstitch in place. Turn a 1cm (½in) hem in on the remaining three sides and press neatly. Topstitch the pocket onto the poncho, reinforcing the corners with stitched triangles.

8. Make four shoulder straps from the contrast fabric. Each one is cut 5cm (2in) wide and 55cm (22in) long. Fold in half down the length and press, then fold the raw edges into the centre and press again. Topstitch close to the fold then knot one end of each shoulder strap. Attach the shoulder straps securely at the outer edges of the neckline. Tie in a bow once the poncho is on your child.

PROJECT VARIATIONS

- *Make the poncho in towelling only. If you did this you will still need to bind the neck. Turn under a double hem around the bottom edge or bind it to match the neck.*

- *Add a simple hood by folding a 50x25cm (20x10in) piece of towelling in half. Add a double 2.5cm (1in) hem around the front edge and attach before binding the neck edge.*

- *Add seaside-inspired appliqués to the hem of the poncho: seashell shapes, starfish or seaweed would look fabulous!*

- *Make the poncho larger or smaller by increasing the width and/or length. You might struggle to get your 15-year-old into a beach poncho but you never know!*

GLOSSARY

APPLIQUÉ One piece of fabric fused and/or stitched on top of another to decorate or embellish.

BACKING The reverse-side of a quilt or quilted craft, usually a whole piece of cotton fabric.

BASTING, or tacking, involves temporarily holding layers of fabric together, usually with a running stitch.

BASTING SPRAY A special kind of spray adhesive used to temporarily hold together the layers of a quilt while the quilting is done.

BATTING, or quilt wadding, is the inner layer of a quilt, which gives it warmth and thickness.

BIAS Fabric cut at a 45-degree to the selvedge, giving the fabric extra stretch.

BINDING A folded strip of fabric used to cover the raw edges on a quilt.

BLANKET STITCH A decorative hand or machine stitch used to neaten appliqué edges.

BOX PLEAT A full pleat formed on the wrong side of the fabric.

CALICO A plain, unbleached wide cotton fabric, useful for backings and cushion inners.

CASING The channel through which elastic, cord or ribbon may be passed for gathering.

COTTON A natural fibre derived from the cotton plant; this fabric or thread is generally soft and inexpensive, washes and wears well, and is easy to sew. Patchwork quilts are generally made of 100% cotton fabrics.

CURTAIN WEIGHT A small weight placed inside a pocket at the hem of curtains and tablecloths to ensure they hang properly.

CUTTING MAT A self-healing cutting mat is used with a rotary cutter and ruler for fabric cutting.

FRAYING When the edges of cut fabric sheds fibres/thread and unravels.

FUSIBLE WEB A sheet of 'glue' attached to paper used for fusible appliqué and for holding hems without sewing.

GRAIN The lengthways and crossways direction of the woven threads in fabric that give fabric its stability.

HEADING TAPE Tapes come in various widths and styles and are stitched to the top of curtains and drawn up to create the gathers.

HEM ALLOWANCE (see also seam allowance) The amount of fabric allowed in the pattern for turning in raw edges or sewing hems and seams.

INTERFACING A layer of special fabric added to another to provide extra strength and structure. Interfacings come in different weights, can be fusible or non-fusible and woven or non-woven.

LINEN A natural fibre made from the flax plant, extremely hard wearing and durable, relatively easy to sew and comes in various weights. Often mixed with other fibres as 'linen union'.

LONGARM QUILTING A method whereby a quilt top is layered and quilted professionally, using a special sewing machine.

MITRE A diagonal seam or fold, usually at a 45-degree angle.

OVERLOCK OR OVERLOCK STITCH A machine stitch that neatens raw edges and prevents or reduces fraying.

PATCHWORK Sewing pieces of fabric together in a random or controlled pattern to create a new, larger piece of fabric. Patchwork is sewn together using a 0.5cm (¼in) seam allowance.

PENCIL PLEAT The most commonly-used type of curtain heading tape.

PINKING SHEARS Scissors that have a special serrated edge, which when used create a zig zag pattern, and can be decorative or used to prevent fraying.

PIPING Generally refers to a fabric covered soft cord inserted into seams on soft furnishings, to both decorate and strengthen them.

PLEAT A fold or tuck of fabric used to shape fabric and add decoration.

PRESSER FOOT The part of a sewing machine that is lowered onto the fabric to hold it while it is stitched. Different feet have different functions.

QUARTER INCH FOOT A sewing machine presser foot used to sew patchwork accurately.

QUILTING Refers to the stitches that hold the layers of a quilt together.

RIGHT SIDE Refers to the outer side of fabric, the printed/decorative or 'pretty' side.

ROTARY CUTTER A round blade on a handle used to cut fabric; always use in conjunction with a self-healing mat and a rotary cutting ruler.

ROTARY RULER A thick perspex ruler marked with either cm or inch markings, used in conjunction with a rotary cutter and self-healing mat.

RUNNING STITCH An evenly spaced stitch with equally spaced gaps, used for basting and gathering fabric layers.

SEAM ALLOWANCE The amount of fabric allowed in a pattern for sewing the pieces together.

SELVEDGE The finished edge on woven fabrics. The selvedge usually carries the manufacturer's name.

STRAIGHT STITCH The most commonly used stitch on a sewing machine, consisting of equal sized stitches on the top and bottom, and without gaps.

TAILOR'S CHALK A triangular piece of chalk used for temporarily marking fabrics. Marks can be easily removed with a brush.

TAPE MEASURE A flexible type of ruler in cm and inches, generally made of fabric.

TOWELLING An absorbent fabric with loops or pile on one side. Generally made of cotton but bamboo is now available.

VELCRO A two part fastening system that consists of a 'hook' side and a 'loop' side – useful for making quick fastenings instead of buttons or zips.

WADDING, or batting, is the inner layer of a quilt, which gives it warmth and thickness.

WALKING FOOT A special presser foot that allows multiple bulky layers to be sewn together. Very useful for machine quilting.

WOOL A natural fibre made from the sheared fleece of sheep, wool is extremely hard wearing, crease resistant and comes in a variety of weights. It is ideal for upholstery.

WRONG SIDE Refers to the reverse side of fabric, the unprinted or 'plain' side.

ZIG ZAG STITCH A machine stitch most often used to neaten cut fabric edge and to prevent fraying (see also overlocking) but may also be used to neaten and decorate the edges of appliqué.

ZIP A fastening system consisting of two tapes held together with interlocking metal or plastic 'teeth'. Zips come in a variety of styles, lengths and colours.

ZIPPER FOOT A narrow presser foot that allows the sewing machine needle to sew very close to the zip teeth.

STOCKISTS

Here are some of my very favourite places to shop for fabric, notions, tools and equipment.

MATERIALS

Soft Body acrylic paint
Liquitex
www.liquitex.com/SoftBody/

505 quilt basting spray
ODIF USA
www.odifusa.com

Velcro hook-and-look self-adhesive tape
Velcro
www.velcro.co.uk

Insul-bright quilt wadding
The Warm Company
www.warmcompany.com

Fast2fuse Fusible interfacing
The Cotton Patch
www.cottonpatch.co.uk

FABRICS

Patchwork and quilting
The Cotton Patch
www.cottonpatch.co.uk

Lady Sew and Sew Fabrics
www.ladysewandsew.co.uk

Free Spirit Fabrics
www.freespiritfabric.com

Deckchair fabrics
Deckchair Stripes
www.deckchairstripes.com

Wool fabrics
Moon
www.moons.co.uk

HABERDASHERY

John Lewis
www.johnlewis.com

Dunelm
www.dunelm-mill.com

MACHINES

Sewing machines
Bernina
www.bernina.com

Quilting machines
Handi Quilter
www.handiquilter.com

INDEX

air-vanishing pens 24
appliqué 14, 16, 24, 27, 33
  aprons 108, 109–10
  bags 86, 201, 208
  bunting 179
  curtains 116
  fusible 16, 20, 22, 34–5
  napkins 99
  personalising gifts 200, 201
  pillowcases 150
  place mats and settings 118, 134
  poncho 215
  quilts 170
  table runner 135–6
  thread 14
aprons
  child's 109–10
  cook's 106–8

baby quilt 170
bagging out 53
bags
  beauty 209–10
  craft 210
  gadget 206–8
  laundry 152–4
  pyjama 152–4
  sewing 210
  tote 96–8
  wash 206–8
batting 17
beach poncho 214–15
beanbag lounger 182–4
beauty bag 209–10
bed valance 159–60
bias strips for binding, cutting 32

binding
  machine sewn 48
  quilts 49–52, 119
blanket stitch 20
bolster cushions 87–8
box-pleated bed valance 159–60
bunting 178–9
buttonholes 20, 164
buttons 16, 18

café curtains 115–16
calico 12
canvas 12
chairs
  revamped dining room 124
  see also deckchair
child's apron 109–10
coat hangers 74–5
conversion chart 217
cook's apron 106–8
cotton fabric 12
craft bag 210
curtains
  café 115–16
  simple lined 84–6
cushion pads 164
cushions
  bolster 87–8
  kitchen seat 112–14
  patchwork 82–3, 146–8
  piped 80
  quilted 162–4, 165, 170
cutlery roll, picnic set 190–2
cutting 5

deckchair 185–8
drawstring laundry bag 152–4
drying cloths, revamped 104

eco shopping tote bag 96–8
edges
  finishing 36
  straightening 31
embellished pillowcases 149–50
embroidery 22, 99, 150, 158, 170, 200
envelope backs 55
everyday place mats 118–19
eye mask 156–8
  pattern 58

fabric-embellished place cards 126
fabrics 5, 12
  straightening edges 31
faux headboard 142
feather cushion pads 164
fibrefill cushion pads 164
floor cloth, painted 68–70
fragrant coat hangers 74–5
fusible appliqué 34–5
fusible webs 16

gadget bag 206–8
gadget covers 204
garden quilt 194
garden windmills 176
glossary 216
glue guns 27
golden rules 5

hammers 27
hanging sleeves 54

headboard 142
headrest, deckchair 188
holdall, deckchair 188
hot glue guns 27
hot pads 101–2

interfacing 16

kitchen seat cushions 112–14
kitchen towels, revamped 104

laminates 12, 22
laundry bag 152–4

marking pencils 24
men's gadget or wash bag 206–8
mitres 43

napkins 99, 130, 190–2
needles 24
noticeboard 64–5

oilcloth 12
overlock stitch 20, 33

painted floor cloth 68–70
patchwork
  cushions 82–3, 146–8
  eye mask 156–8
  laundry/pyjama bag 152–4
  quilt 165–8
patterns
  in envelope
  eye mask 58
  spoon appliqué 59
personalising gifts 200

picnic set 190–2
pieced backings 53
pillowcases 144–5, 149–50
pins 24
piping 37–9
place cards 126
place mats 46, 118–19, 190–2
place settings 132–4
poncho 214–15
pyjama bag 152–4

quilted cushion 162–4, 165, 170
quilting 18, 48, 164, 168
   basting spray 17, 47
   layering 46–7
   wadding 17
quilts
   baby 170
   binding 49–52, 119
   garden 194
   patchwork 165–8

rectangles, cutting 32
revamped deckchair 185–8
revamped dining room chairs 124
revamped kitchen towels/drying cloths 104
revamped picture frame noticeboard 64–5
rotary cutters 27, 31
rulers 27

scented heart sachets 75, 202
scissors 27
scraps 14
seams, sewing 33
seasonal wreath 66–7
self-healing mats 27, 31
sewing 5
sewing bag 210
sewing machines 18
   interchangeable feet 22–3

shoe tidy, hanging 71–3
simple lined curtains 84–6
simple piped cushion 80
simple tablecloth 127–8
sofa throw 90
splash-proof gadget covers 204
spoon appliqué, pattern 59
squares, cutting 32
staple guns 27
stitches 20, 33
stockists 218
straight stitch 20, 33
strips, cutting 32
sun hat 212–13
suppliers 218

table runner 135–6
tablecloth 127–8
tabs 40–1
tailor's chalk 24
tape measures 24
thermal insulating wadding 17
thread 14
throw 90
ties 40–1
tools/equipment 5
tote bag, eco shopping 96–8
triangles, cutting 32
trims 16

upholstery fabric 12
upholstery tacks/pins 27

wadding 17, 164
wash bag 206–8
windmills 176
wool 12

zigzag stitch 20, 33
zips, inserting 44–5

ACKNOWLEDGEMENTS

Just like the sewing bees of old, this book is a collaboration and required many hands to create it. I want to say a heartfelt thanks to everyone who has been involved.

To Heather and all at HHB for being brave and setting off on this journey with me, to Amanda, my publisher, for believing in both me and the concept of *Sew Fabulous*, and huge thanks also to Abi, Jillian, Lucie, LouLou, Dan, Andrew and Giuliana, for creating a book of such beauty.

Thanks must also go to my parents, friends and most of all, my partner, Charlie, who have all encouraged, supported and inspired me to aim so high. Without your love and belief none of this would have been possible.

Finally, to Miss Jenkins, my teacher, a wonderful lady who believed in everyone's creativity – my gratitude.

I hope you will find the same inspiration in these pages.

Stuart
xxx

To Charlie, who makes life fabulous!

First published in Great Britain in 2014
by Weidenfeld & Nicolson,
an imprint of The Orion Publishing Group Ltd

Orion House
Upper St Martin's Lane
London WC2H 9EA
An Hachette UK Company

Photographer: Dan Jones
Illustrator: Kuo Kang Chen
Design and Art direction: Abi Hartshorne
Stylist: Giuliana Casarotti
Project editor: Jillian Young
Copy editor: Clare Sayer
Proofreader: Elise See Tai
Indexer: Elizabeth Wiggans

A CIP catalogue record for this book is available from the British Library.

ISBN: 978-0-297-87132-3

The Orion Publishing Group's policy is to use papers that are natural, renewable
and recyclable and made from wood grown in sustainable forests. The logging and
manufacturing processes are expected to conform to environmental regulations of the
country of origin.

www.orionbooks.co.uk